体验世界文化之旅阅读文库 新加坡

Singapore
Culture Smart!

Angela Milligan 著
邵春美 注

按照姓氏拼音排序
文库总策划
贾巍巍

文库主编
王守仁 仲伟合

文库副主编
李淑静 石坚 王艳 赵雯

分册主编
仲伟合

高等教育出版社·北京

图字：01-2015-8228号

Culture Smart! Singapore, by Angela Milligan, first published by Kuperard Publishing, a publishing imprint of Bravo Ltd.

Culture Smart!® is a registered trademark of Bravo Ltd. All rights reserved.

Copyright © 2004 Kuperard

Cover image:Merlion statue, Singapore.
Travel Ink/Geoffrey Clive

图书在版编目（CIP）数据

新加坡：英文／（英）安吉拉·米里根（Angela Milligan）著；仲伟合主编；邵春美注. -- 北京：高等教育出版社，2017.3
（体验世界文化之旅阅读文库／王守仁，仲伟合主编）
书名原文：Singapore-Culture Smart!
ISBN 978-7-04-046975-2

Ⅰ. ①新… Ⅱ. ①安… ②仲… ③邵… Ⅲ. ①新加坡-概况-英文 Ⅳ. ①K933.9

中国版本图书馆CIP数据核字(2016)第318925号

策划编辑	刘 瑾	项目编辑	刘 瑾	责任编辑	陈锡镖	封面设计	张 楠
版式设计	孙 伟	责任校对	叶春阳	责任印制	赵义民		

出版发行	高等教育出版社	网　　址	http://www.hep.edu.cn
社　　址	北京市西城区德外大街4号		http://www.hep.com.cn
邮政编码	100120	网上订购	http://www.hepmall.com.cn
印　　刷	北京中科印刷有限公司		http://www.hepmall.com
开　　本	880 mm×1230 mm　1/32		http://www.hepmall.cn
印　　张	7		
字　　数	169千字	版　　次	2017年3月第1版
购书热线	010-58581118	印　　次	2017年3月第1次印刷
咨询电话	400-810-0598	定　　价	39.00元

本书如有缺页、倒页、脱页等质量问题，请到所购图书销售部门联系调换
版权所有　侵权必究
物料号　46975-00

出版说明

为服务"一带一路"国家战略，促进不同文化互鉴共荣，我们引进改编了英国普拉德出版社（Kuperard Publishing）*Culture Smart!* 及 *Simple Guides* 系列丛书，隆重推出"体验世界文化之旅阅读文库"，将带您探索不同的文化，跨越因文化差异造成的交际障碍，领略绚丽多彩的异国风情。

本文库内容涉及五大洲近100个国家的独特文化，填补了非欧美等发达国家相关信息缺失的空白。在编排上，同一系列内部采用相同的体例；既可单册阅读，也能满足专题研究和地域文化横向比较的需要。我们约请国内专家团队对文库进行了改编：对疑难词汇、文化现象进行了注释，增加了名人轶事和名校介绍，更新了过时信息；此外，还围绕每个章节的关键事实设计了练习题，以便读者加深记忆和查阅相关信息。

特别要提醒广大读者的是，文化本身属于一个不断发展的范畴。为了增进来自不同文化背景的人们之间的交流和理解，有必要对各国的文化差异进行一定程度的概括，而对文化定势的概括一方面蕴含着准确的文化观察，另一方面也可能出现主观的文化迁移。只有不囿于文化定势，在实践中不断摸索，才能推动跨文化沟通的顺利进行。由于本文库作者的文化背景、观念和个性迥异，他们在描写各国基本国情、历史文化、世俗风情等方面时，难免流露些许个人的偏见，我们本着建立和谐世界的愿望，对一些偏激之言酌情作了处理；我们尊重作者的表达，但作者的某些看法并不代表我们的观点，需要读者予以分析明辨。此外，文库中涉及的有关数据请以中华人民共和国外交部最新公布的数据为准。

就此让心释然，让我们一起体验旅不问人、行随己意的世界文化之旅吧！

高等教育出版社
2017年2月

总　序

在我们这个星球上，有 70 多亿人口，200 多个国家和地区，2,500 多个民族，5,000 多种语言。在地理位置、历史传统、思想文化等因素的形塑下，人们的生活方式、社会风俗、思维模式、审美情趣、价值观念等呈现出不同特点。在纪念孔子诞辰 2,565 周年国际学术研讨会上，国家主席习近平指出："不同国家、民族的思想文化各有千秋，只有姹紫嫣红之别而无高低优劣之分。每个国家、每个民族不分强弱、不分大小，其思想文化都应该得到承认和尊重。"

在经济全球化和科技进步的推动下，中国与世界的命运更加紧密地联系在一起。截至 2016 年 3 月和我国建交的国家多达 173 个，随着"一带一路"战略的提出与实施，我国与非英美文化国家的交往日益频繁。在我们大踏步走向世界的过程中，迫切需要了解各个国家的情况，了解各国的人民及其文化。目前国内出版的介绍外国国情的英语书籍大多限于英、美等发达国家，涉及其他国家概况的英语出版物寥寥无几。

为服务"一带一路"国家战略，促进各国人民的人文交流与文明互鉴，高等教育出版社引进英国 Kuperard 出版社 *Culture Smart!* 及 *Simple Guides* 系列丛书，编辑出版"体验世界文化之旅阅读文库"。本文库共 96 册，其中亚洲国家 28 册、欧洲国家 31 册、美洲国家 16 册、非洲国家 14 册、大洋洲国家 2 册，含"一带一路"沿线国家 45 册；另有一单独画册与科学系列和哲学系列丛书各 2 册。

"体验世界文化之旅阅读文库"用世界的眼光、易懂的语言、深入的剖析为学习者展示出一幅幅多姿多彩的世界各国风情画卷。每册简述相关国家社会文化的基本方面和主要线索，既有关于各国地理、历史、政治、国民性格、信仰、态度和行为习惯的描述，也有对普通人家庭生活、工作和娱乐、饮食特色、商业文化、社交礼仪的介绍。本文库为广大读者提供认识各国社会文化的一把钥匙，为那些准备出国交流、学习、旅游或工作的学习者提供基本的帮助和实用的工具性指南。学习者在阅读的过程中不仅可以知晓相关国家的风土人情，还能了解深层次的文化传统和价值观念，提高对文化差异的敏感度和宽容度，提升跨文化交际的能力。

本文库除国别系列之外，*Culture Smart!* 系列还单独有一画册《世界节日大观》，用 270 幅彩色照片，配以生动的说明文字，呈现世界各地包括巴西里约热内卢的狂欢节和印度阿拉哈巴德的宗教圣节"大壶节"在内的节日瞬间，让读者直观地了解精彩各异的地域文化。*Simple Guides* 系列中，哲学系列丛书展示人类思想发展历史和不同哲学传统；科学系列丛书介绍改变世界的伟大发现和发明创造，能帮助读者加深对我们所生活的世界的认识。

总序

"体验世界文化之旅阅读文库"英语简洁明了、难度适中,语言地道,可供大学生课外阅读。对于英语基础较好、不满足大学英语四、六级水平的非英语专业学生而言,"体验世界文化之旅阅读文库"将不失为习得世界不同国家文化的理想读本。对英语类专业的学生而言,本文库也可拓展学习者的国际视野,增加其跨文化交际知识。尽可能多地接触英语,是学好英语的有效方法,而大量阅读可以培养语感、扩大词汇量、提高理解能力。"体验世界文化之旅阅读文库"可以为广大读者提高英语水平助力。在国家实施"走出去"发展战略之际,"体验世界文化之旅阅读文库"将伴随我们去认识世界、走向世界。

让我们开始体验世界文化之旅,享受英语、享受阅读!

王守仁
2016 年 6 月

分册序

新加坡在你的脑海里是怎样的呢？适合游玩？商场里多是夏季的衣服出售？乱丢垃圾也要罚款？不能用左手吃饭和握手？其实禁忌不止这些，本书将带您走进一个真正的新加坡，让您从各方面深入了解新加坡。

新加坡是马来半岛最南端的一个岛国，自1965年8月9日宣布独立以来，迅速发展为全球高度现代化的国家之一。国旗为星月旗，国徽由盾徽、狮子和老虎等组成，国花为胡姬花，象征新加坡人果敢奋斗的精神。

多元文化的和谐发展、廉洁高效的政府、良好的治安、缤纷的美景和整洁的市容使旅游者心生向往，旅游业成为新加坡经济的支柱产业之一。阿拉伯风情街和小印度浓郁的民族风情，圣淘沙岛和新加坡动物园活力十足，莱佛士酒店和旧议会大厦历史悠久，新加坡演绎着传统与现代的完美结合。特色美食和商圈也是新加坡的一大特色，新加坡拥有完善的公共交通体系，现代高效的地铁系统是出行首选。

新加坡是典型的城市国家，又名"狮城""花园城市"，旧称"星洲"，法律的严酷使得新加坡的犯罪率较低，并维持了整个城市的清洁环境。在这里可以体会各种文化的交融与和平共处，多种族与多宗教使新加坡呈现出一种别样的生机。崇尚以目标为导向，新加坡人有一种"怕输"的心理，这使得新加坡人在处事时体现出讲求实效的精英特质。自宣布独立以来，李光耀带领新加坡人走出了一条属于自己的道路，时至今日，李光耀的影响仍然深刻，尤其是在政治、语言和教育方面。新加坡人一方面秉承亚洲的传统价值观，另一方面各民族也拥有自己独特的风俗习惯，在这样一个年轻而富有活力的移民国家中，和谐成为最大的亮点。英语、汉语、马来语和泰米尔语是新加坡宪法规定的四种官方语言，彰显了其多元文化特色，几乎每个新加坡人都会说至少两种语言。

中国与新加坡两国素有历史和文化渊源，一直保持着友好往来的关系，如苏州工业园区是两国政府重要的国际合作项目。新加坡是东盟的主要经济体，而中国是东盟的最大贸易伙伴，"一带一路"战略的实施必将会为两国在多领域的合作提供更多的机会。对新加坡的文化、历史、政治等的全方位了解既是跨文化交流的需要，也是为经贸发展奠定良好基础的要求。新加坡全球重要的金融中心地位有利于其在"一带一路"的融资活动中发挥作用，中国与新加坡的合作也会因此而向多方位拓展。

本书作者安吉拉·米里根 (Angela Milligan) 毕业于东英吉利大学历史专业，现专门为意欲移居国外的人提供以文化意识等为主题的培训。作者曾旅居东亚多国、澳大利亚、比利时和阿根廷等地,并为新加坡的主要跨国公司做过推介,因此对新加坡的风土人情有较为深刻的感受。本书将带您畅游新加坡,在了解当地风土人情的基础上深入体会多元文化的融合——从地理概况、人文风貌、价值观、风俗习惯、饮食文化、商务沟通等方面全景展示一个真实的新加坡,能够使读者融入其中,做到"入乡随俗"。同时文中的加注释有助于提高阅读效率,书后的开放式思考题有助于读者在阅读中思考,提高批判式阅读能力,习题可以帮助读者在词汇、文化、理解能力及表述能力等方面有所提高。

邵春美

2016 年 12 月

Contents

Singapore 001
Introduction 002
Key Facts 004

Chapter 01 **LAND & PEOPLE** 006
- Climate *007*
- Flora and Fauna *008*
- The People *009*
- A Brief History *018*
- Lee Kuan Yew *030*
- Social Change *031*
- Law and Order *036*
- Political Life *037*
- Low Population Growth *039*

Chapter 02 **VALUES & ATTITUDES** 042
- Common Asian Values *042*
- Religion *044*
- The Chinese *045*
- The Malays *055*
- The Indians *059*
- Education *061*
- A Goal-Driven Society *064*

Chapter 03   **CUSTOMS & TRADITIONS**   **065**
- Festivals and Holidays   *065*
- The Chinese Lunar Calendar   *073*
- Births   *075*
- Weddings   *077*
- Funerals   *081*
- Gift Giving   *084*

Chapter 04   **THE SINGAPOREANS AT HOME**   **090**
- Social and Family Relationships   *090*
- Children   *091*
- Lifestyle and Housing   *093*
- Invitations Home   *093*
- Greetings   *096*
- Public Display   *097*
- Boy Meets Girl   *098*
- National Service   *100*
- Names   *101*

Chapter 05   **FOOD & DRINK**   **107**
- Cooking Styles   *111*
- Dietary Restrictions   *112*
- Food Courts   *114*
- Drink   *115*

Contents
iii

Chapter 06 **TIME OUT** 117
- Tourism *117*
- Getting Around *118*
- MRT *118*
- Destinations *122*
- Rules and Regulations *131*
- Money *132*
- Safety *133*
- Shopping *134*
- Nightlife *137*
- Culture *139*

Chapter 07 **BANQUETS & ENTERTAINING** 142
- Eating Etiquette *142*
- Seating Arrangements *145*
- Making Speeches and Proposing Toasts *146*
- Reciprocating *147*

Chapter 08 **BUSINESS BRIEFING** 151
- The Economic Miracle *151*
- Financial Management *154*
- Building Relationships *156*
- Introductions *157*
- Small Talk *158*
- Hands *159*

- Business Cards *159*
- Meetings *160*
- Women in Business *162*
- Saving Face *163*
- Negotiating Styles *165*
- Decision Making *167*
- Contracts and Fulfillment *168*
- Team Building *168*

Chapter 09 COMMUNICATING **171**

- Telecommunications *171*
- The Internet *172*
- The Media *173*
- Postal Services *175*
- Languages *176*
- Body Language *184*
- Humor *186*
- Conclusion *187*

Appendices **188**

- Places *188*
- People *192*

Exercises **195**

Singapore

1 资产
2 优先考虑的事
3 充满活力的
4 和左邻右舍比排场、比阔气
5 闽南话，福建话
6 被遗忘

Introduction

The small island state of Singapore is unique in the region. Not only is it a very young country — independence came in 1965 — but it is a land of immigrants, in which people from three distinct backgrounds, Chinese, Malay, and Indian, live side by side in harmony.

Singapore's multicultural harmony is no accident. From the beginning, realizing that its people were its most precious asset[1], the government made free education for all a national priority[2], with schools teaching positive attitudes as well as essential knowledge and skills. This is an energetic[3], "can do" society, whose citizens are often worried about not keeping up with the Joneses[4], or, as it is portrayed in Singapore, "*kiasu*," from the Hokkien[5] word meaning "to miss out[6]."

On August 9, 1965, the national leader Lee Kuan Yew faced the unknown when he announced that Singapore had been forced to leave the newly formed Federation of Malaysia. Many commentators feared the worst, for this newly created republic had no natural resources, was tiny compared to its neighbors, and only had its deep water harbor, its commercial skills, and its close proximity to the rest of Asia to rely on. Within fifteen years, however, Singapore had transformed itself

Introduction

into an economic powerhouse[1] and become a byword[2] for technical excellence.

Yet despite its Western veneer[3], the visitor is quickly reminded that the "Lion City" is most definitely Asian. Although many of the traditional cultural values of the communities living there have been challenged by the demands of the modern Singaporean state, their underlying philosophies remain intact. It is therefore difficult to talk about a typical Singaporean, for this would depend on whether one was referring to someone of Chinese, Malay, or Indian descent. By and large, however, this is a very goal-oriented, meritocratic[4] society. It is also fair to say that the three ethnic groups share certain Asian values — belief in ordered relationships, obligation, respect for traditions, polite behavior, and the protection of face, both for oneself and for others.

Culture Smart! Singapore introduces the foreign visitors to the rich and varied cultures and customs of Singapore's communities. It shows what motivates people, how they interact with each other and with outsiders, and tells you what to expect and how to behave in unfamiliar situations. In doing so, it offers you a fuller, more rounded experience of this fascinating society.

[1] 强国
[2] 代名词
[3] 外饰面，表层
[4] 精英管理的

Key Facts

Official Name	Republic of Singapore	Singapore is a member of ASEAN.
Capital	Singapore City	On the southeast coast of the Island.
Area	244 sq miles (633 sq km), virtually all urban[1].	
Currency	Singapore Dollar	
Climate	Tropical, hot 73°–90°F (23°–32°C), humid and rainy all year.	There is a monsoon[2] season from November to January.
Population	2015: 5.535 million; 19% nonresident.	
Ethnic Makeup	Chinese 75% with the remaining Malay, Indian and other ethnic groups	
Religion	Buddhism, Taoism, Islam, Hinduism, Sikhism, Christianity, Judaism	Freedom of religion is enshrined in the Constitution.
Official Languages	Chinese (Mandarin), Malay, Tamil, English	Malay is the national language. English is the language of administration and business.
Government	Parliamentary republic, ruled by the People's Action Party since independence. Head of State: President Tony Tan Keng Yam; Prime Minister: **Lee Hsien Loong**.	Cabinet appointed by the prime minister and responsible to parliament. The president is elected by popular vote for six years. Elections to unicameral[3] parliament held every five years.

[1] 根据中华人民共和国外交部网站截至 2016 年 12 月公布的最新数据，新加坡截至 2015 年的领土面积为 719.1 平方公里
[2] 雨季
[3] （议会）一院制的

Key Facts

Adult Literacy	98% male, 88% female	Literacy in 2 or more languages 56%
Family Makeup	Average number of children per family: 1.24 Infant mortality rate: 4 per 1000 births	Age structure: 0–14 years 17%; 15–64 years 76%; 65 years and over 7%. Population growth: 1.8% per annum resident; 9% nonresident. Life expectancy: 77 years male, 84 years female.
Economy[1]	Most prosperous in Asia in terms of per capita GDP. Much of the economy is based on importing and reexporting and financial services.	Exports: electronics, manufactures, and chemicals. GDP growth rate flat in 2000–2002; picking up with 0.8% in 2003.
Media	Both local and international newspapers and television channels are available.	Restrictions sometimes apply where international newspapers and magazines are highly critical of the government or its policies.
Electricity	220–240 volts/ 50 Hz	
Internet Domain	.sg	
Telephone	International country code: 65	
Time Difference	GMT + 8 hours	

[1] 2014年，新加坡国民经济增长2.8%，2015年增长2%，人均收入突破6万美元

Chapter 01

LAND & PEOPLE

Singapore is a small island state at the southern end of the Malay Peninsula[1]. Separated by narrowstraits from mainland Malaysia, and by the Straits of Malacca[2] from Sumatra[3], one of the largest islands in the Indonesian archipelago[4], it is approximately 20 miles (32 km) long east-west and 12 miles (20 km) wide north-south. It consists of fifty-nine islands and has a population of 5.47 million people.

Singapore City, on the southeast coast of the island, is dominated by tall skyscrapers, some taller than the island's highest point, Bukit Timah Hill[5]. The modern buildings contain smart offices, numerous hotels, and glamorous shops. Yet despite

[1] 马来半岛，又叫克拉半岛或马六甲半岛，位于亚洲东南部。马来半岛包括泰国的西南部、马来西亚的西部和新加坡，自古以来是联系经济和文化的枢纽

[2] 马六甲海峡，位于马来西亚和苏门答腊之间，现由新加坡、马来西亚和印度尼西亚三国共同管辖

[3] 苏门答腊，印度尼西亚第二大岛屿，东北隔马六甲海峡与马来半岛相望。自古以来苏门答腊山区出产黄金，因此也被称为金洲

[4] 印度尼西亚群岛，世界上最大的群岛，包含17,000多个岛屿，从印度洋的苏门答腊岛直至太平洋的哈马黑拉岛

[5] 武吉知马山，新加坡海拔最高点，热带雨林保护区

Land & People

the predominance[1] of buildings, great thought and effort have gone into keeping the city green. You are immediately aware of this on the drive into the city from the airport — the long, straight road is lined with colorful bougainvilleas[2] and frangipani[3] as well as travelers' palms[4] and jacarandas[5]. This is possibly the best drive from an airport into a capital city anywhere in the world, as these are usually rather nondescript[6], if not downright[7] grim, stretches of highway in most countries.

[1] 优势，占主导地位
[2] 九重葛属植物
[3] 赤素馨，鸡蛋花
[4] 旅人蕉
[5] 蓝花楹属树
[6] 无特征的，平庸的，毫无特色的
[7] 完全的

CLIMATE

The climate is tropical. Situated just 50 north of the equator, Singapore is either hot and sticky or very hot and sticky all year round. The monsoon weather, which lasts from November to January, brings heavy rain and occasional flooding, but this does lower the temperature from 86°F (30°C) to 73°F (23°C). The hottest and most humid months are from March to July — but expect dramatic thunderstorms at any time of the year. Be warned, though: many visitors catch cold, owing to the contrast of the outside temperature with the

Chapter 01

1 动植物
2 紫白色的兰花
3 兰花，东南亚人习惯称为胡姬花
4 杂交品种
5 新加坡植物园，著名旅游景点
6 小饰品
7 气候
8 万里胡姬花公园，是新加坡最著名的园艺旅游圣地之一，展示了包括新加坡国花在内的多种胡姬花，包括古香花园、水上花园和热带水果园
9 马来亚，是马亚西亚西部的旧称，又名西马来

aggressive air conditioning in some hotels and restaurants.

FLORA AND FAUNA[1]

Singapore's national flower is the purple and white orchid[2] "Vanda Miss Joaquim[3]," a natural hybrid[4] discovered in the garden of the lady of that name and subsequently presented to the Botanical Gardens[5]. You will see the national emblem everywhere, from tourist trinkets[6] and politicians' shirts to the carefully packed bunches on sale at the airport for travelers to take back to colder climes[7] as a souvenir of exotic Southeast Asia. Singapore exports large quantities of these flowers, and the Mandai Orchid Gardens[8], with over two hundred species, are well worth a visit, as are the Singapore Botanic Gardens. These gardens make up the oldest public park in Singapore and are famous for being the birthplace of the region's rubber industry. This brought great wealth to the area — to Malaya[9] for growing it and to the port of Singapore for its export.

There is a nature reserve at Bukit Timah

Hill. This is Singapore's last remaining pocket of primary rain forest, and has an abundance of plant species. It is also the location of the island's highest point. Many visitors like to stroll to the peak to see the monkeys; this is best done either in the cool of the early morning or in the evening, avoiding the hottest times of the day.

Similarly, the best time to visit the Sungei Buloh Wetland Reserve[1] on the north coast is in the early morning. This protected wetland nature park becomes a stopover[2] point from November to March for migrating birds from as far away as Eastern Siberia[3]. You can observe the birds in their natural environment from hides.

THE PEOPLE

Singapore is a land of immigrants. Apart from small coastal communities, it was virtually uninhabited until the nineteenth century, when Britain turned it into a strategic naval and commercial staging post, triggering substantial immigration, particularly from China. More of a salad bowl than a melting pot, the resulting society

[1] 双溪布洛湿地保护区，位于新加坡西北部，占地87公顷，是重要的自然保护区，也是唯一受保护的沼泽自然公园，独特的候鸟群是其特色之一
[2] 中途停留
[3] 东西伯利亚

Chapter 01

[1] 泰米尔语，是达罗毗荼语系中最重要的语言，新加坡法定官方语言之一，也是印度宪法承认的语言之一，斯里兰卡的官方语言之一

[2] 沉重的，压迫的

is a model of multicultural harmony. Although the Chinese are by far the largest ethnic group, the Malays who make up just over 14 percent of the population, and the Indians who form 8 percent, contribute more to Singaporean society than their numbers would suggest.

The official languages of Singapore are therefore Malay (which is also the "national" language), Chinese (Mandarin), Tamil[1], and English. English is the language of administration, business, and technology.

The Chinese Immigrants

Life in China in the last days of the Qing dynasty in the nineteenth century was harsh and oppressive[2] for many. Poverty was widespread and those in the coastal provinces did not need much invitation to leave. The first junk bound for Singapore with migrants sailed from Amoy[1] in 1821, and by 1827 the local Malay population was vastly outnumbered[2].

The British encouraged this immigration, as the Chinese were reckoned to be a hardy and industrious people. Many were illiterate and penniless, but once they had paid off their passage they flourished. Some came as indentured[3] laborers to work in the tin mines of Malaya and the docks in Singapore. They became coolies[4], farmers, and traders.

Their numbers continued to grow, even though the Singapore government tried to impose quotas, especially during the years of the Great Depression. The administration was always anxious to maintain a balance between the sexes and so avoided the problem of prostitution[5] that had occurred in the early years of the nineteenth century when most of the immigrants were young men. In the early years of the twentieth century, there were still more men than women: something like 240 men to every 100 women.

1 厦门（旧称）
2 数量超过，比…多
3 受契约束缚的
4 苦力
5 卖淫

Chapter 01

[1] 四个三角洲，分别指流入福州的闽江，厦门的九龙江，汕头附近的韩江以及位于广州南部的珠江
[2] 福州话
[3] 闽南语
[4] 潮州话
[5] 派别活动

Most Overseas Chinese, not just those of Singapore, come from the southern coastal provinces between Hong Kong and Shanghai. Some were original inhabitants of the region and others had migrated south over the centuries. Although they are all Chinese, they come from a number of different ethnic groups. They share the same written language but speak completely different dialects and have different local cultures that they value.

However, most of these ethnic groups trace their origins to four river deltas[1]: the Min River flows into the South China Sea at Fuzhou, the Chiu-lung at Xiamen (Amoy), the Han River near Shantou (Swatow), and the Pearl River south of Guangzhou (Canton) and opposite Hong Kong.

The people from Fuzhou speak Hokchiu[2]; those from Xiamen speak Hokkien[3] (this is the largest ethnic group in Singapore); those from Shantou speak Hoklo[4] (but are called Teochew); and those from the Pearl River delta and Guangzhou call themselves and speak Cantonese. In the early days, this led to factionalism[5] and clan conflicts in Singapore.

The Hakka[1], who speak Hakka, emigrated from Guangdong, Fujian, and Jiangxi provinces, and the Hainanese from Hainan Island, the most southerly part of China that is opposite the Vietnamese coast.

In Singapore today, members of the older generation still speak their native dialects, but increasing numbers of young Chinese people speak Mandarin at home.

Straits Chinese

There was, however, a group of Chinese who came to settle in Singapore who were very different from the poor, illiterate migrants. They were the Straits Chinese, or Chinese who had adopted Malay customs. They were descendants of the old Chinese families of sixteenth-century Malacca and Penang[2]. Over the centuries the Straits Chinese were influenced by their Malay neighbors, and some even felt more comfortable speaking Malay. The women adopted Malay-style dress and were referred to as Nonya[3]. Their cuisine

[1] 客家人，客家话
[2] （马来西亚）槟城
[3] 娘惹，指中国人和马来西亚人通婚的女性后代

Chapter 01

[^1]: 峇峇，指中国人和马来西亚人通婚的男性后代
[^2]: 桌球
[^3]: 了解…的最新进展
[^4]: "中华帝国"，1915年12月至1916年3月袁世凯称帝，后被迫取消帝制
[^5]: 古体的，古代的
[^6]: 腐败的官僚

was transformed by typical Malay ingredients such as fragrant roots, herbs, chilies, and, above all, coconut milk. They combined the traditional love of pork — forbidden, of course, to Malay Muslims — with classic Malay ingredients.

The Straits Chinese were educated, had money, and soon found themselves an indispensable part of the colonial administration. Some became doctors, lawyers, and teachers, while others established successful businesses, especially in the timber and rubber trades. The men, referred to as the Baba community[1], were often ridiculed for being "more British than the British." Their newspapers were in English rather than Chinese, and they adopted the manners of their colonial masters, playing billiards[2] and drinking brandy. Although they did not mix socially with the new Chinese immigrants, they kept abreast of[3] developments on the mainland, especially those to do with the reform of Imperial China[4]'s archaic[5] system of government, conducted by corrupt bureaucrats[6] from northern China. So it comes as no surprise to learn that it was a Straits Chinese,

Teo Eng Hock[1], who offered his large villa to Sun Yat Sen[2], the future first President of China, when he sought refuge in Singapore. You can visit his villa today and view its vast collection of artifacts and photographs, for the Singapore government restored the villa in 1964 to commemorate Sun Yat Sen and his revolutionary nationalist movement.

The Malay Community

The original Malay inhabitants of the island were soon outnumbered by the thousands of Chinese immigrants looking for a better way of life. It is a testament[3] to the strength of their community that not only did it survive intact, but in many ways it influenced the newcomers. Malay is the national language of Singapore, and one of the four official languages. (English, however, is the language of administration.)

    The Malays are a gentle, courteous people — always generous and hospitable. Indeed, together with the promotion of social harmony, these are core Malay values. They have a strong belief in community, no doubt growing out of the

---

[1] 张永福（1872–1957），生于新加坡，孙中山辛亥革命时在海外的主要助手
[2] 孙中山（1866–1925），中国近代伟大的资产阶级革命先行者
[3] 证据

[1] 房地产开发区块
[2] 独立的，依靠自己的

traditional *kampong* (small village) way of life. Although the *kampongs* have been replaced by the ethnically diverse Housing Development Blocks[1], their values still prevail.

The Malays have become self-reliant[2] and have prospered in the new Singapore, owning apartments and holding down good jobs. They do not believe in the pursuit of wealth for its own sake, but in the greater importance of the spiritual side of life. This is reflected in their concern not only for their families but for their neighbors as well.

The Malays want visitors to enjoy Singapore and their particular Malay culture. However, there are still a few "dos and don'ts" that visitors should be aware of, which in turn will make them feel comfortable and not worry about upsetting or embarrassing their hosts. These are discussed in Chapter 4, The Singaporeans at Home, and Chapter 8, Business Briefing.

The Indian Community

Despite making up just over 8 percent of the

population, Indians have always been prominent in politics and the law, possibly because they are passionate public speakers who love arguments. They are also well represented in the other professions, such as commerce and industry.

To get an understanding of the Indian community, it is a good idea to visit "Little India" on Serangoon Road[1]. Some of the shops now have Chinese owners but still sell the traditional colorful wares that their customers demand. Indeed, most Indians still shop there, especially when buying saris, men's dhotis[2], betel nuts[3], heavy brass stands, garlands[4] for weddings, arm bangles[5], and other indispensable items for an Indian household.

Like the Chinese, Indian shopkeepers appreciate a customer who will haggle[6] and who relishes[7] the prospect of a bargain. Again, as with the Chinese, the Indians regard it as a good omen if the first customer of the day buys something, however small, and especially if that purchase includes flowers, sugar, or sweets — but not oil. The latter is regarded as not a good sign for the

[1] 实龙岗路，新加坡最古老的马路之一
[2] 腰布
[3] 槟榔
[4] 花环，花冠
[5] 手镯
[6] 讨价还价
[7] 欣赏

1. 蒲罗中，即马来语"半岛末端的岛屿"的意思，是当时中国对新加坡的称谓
2. 马可波罗（1254–1324），13世纪意大利著名的商人和旅行家
3. 马可波罗游记中对新加坡的称呼
4. 梵文，梵语
5. 暹罗（即今天的泰国）以及位于爪哇岛的满者伯夷帝国（Majapahit Empire）曾经争夺新加坡的控制权
6. 人质，此处指据守点
7. 互相残杀的

rest of the day's trading.

A BRIEF HISTORY

Despite being such a new nation-state, Singapore has a long history, owing to its strategic position at the junction of many shipping routes. There is a mention in 203 CE in the writings of General Lu Tai of the Chinese Emperor's sending an expedition to Pue-lo-Chung[1], as Singapore was then known. Much later, in the closing years of the thirteenth century, Marco Polo[2] visited Sumatra and wrote about a noble city called Chiamassie[3], which historians have identified as Singapore. A hundred or so years later it had changed its name to Singapura, Sanskrit[4] for "Lion City." Nobody knows why it got this name; the reason is lost in the mists of time. The city then went into decline as a result of the rivalry between the expanding Thai and Javanese empires[5]. Singapore's geographical position, which was to be such a bonus six hundred years later, meant that it became a pawn[6] in these internecine[7] wars, and this led to its abandonment when the traders moved to Malacca, which was

Land & People

fortified[1] and much more secure. Only a few people — known as sea people — remained, surviving on fishing and, when times were hard, piracy.

Early Days

Long before the British arrived, the location was favored by traders taking their wares from Arabia, India, and the Malay peninsula to East and Southeast Asia and back again on the seasonal monsoon winds. This activity reached a peak as a port under the Malays in the thirteenth century, but was later curtailed[2] by the Mongols and so it remained until the arrival of Raffles[3].

Colonization

In the eighteenth century Britain and the Netherlands were commercial competitors in the East-West trade, while Britain and France were military enemies and sought to extend their empires in the region. Early in the nineteenth century the French were defeated in Europe and no longer posed a threat to British and Dutch

[1] 设要塞，加固的
[2] 削减，缩短
[3] 托马斯·斯坦福·莱佛士（1781-1826），为英国殖民时期东印度群岛的行政官员，新加坡海港城市的创建人，主要贡献在于将新加坡建立为欧洲和亚洲间的重要国际港口

Chapter 01

[1] 亦称不列颠东印度公司或英国东印度公司，1600年成立，享有英国皇家在印度从事贸易的特许权，实际上还享有政治和军事职能，1858年被解散
[2] 孟加拉，南亚地区，位于孟加拉湾北部
[3] 广州（旧称）
[4] 鸦片
[5] 垄断
[6] 抢购
[7] 大百货商店
[8] 支点
[9] 从何处，从哪里
[10] 新加坡的马来国王（1776–1835）

interests in Asia. The British and the Dutch then set out to acquire exclusive trading posts through agreements with local rulers.

Britain was represented in the region by the powerful East India Company[1] whose commercial strength was backed by its own military force. It had long wanted to have a halfway house between Bengal[2], its power base, and Canton[3], the source of its new wealth in tea and the destination for its opium[4], produced in India, for which the Company had a monopoly.[5] The Dutch were snapping up[6] what seemed the best ports, and Thomas, later Sir Stamford, Raffles of the Company had long wanted to establish a trading post in the region. "Our object is not territory but trade," he wrote, "a great commercial emporium[7] and a fulcrum[8] whence[9] we may extend our influence politically as circumstances may hereafter require." He negotiated a treaty with Sultan Hussein of Johore[10] giving Britain the right to establish a trading post on the island of Singapore and proclaim it a free port, and on February 6, 1819, the Union flag of Great Britain was officially raised. Security and

stability soon attracted ships in search of a safe haven to restock with food and water, and those needing to repair their vessels. Success was almost guaranteed.

Raffles was one of a special breed of freewheeling[1] and adventurous spirits produced by Britain's great commercial empire. However else one views it today, the Empire gave opportunities and scope to many British men of humble birth, many of whom became efficient and fair administrators, humanitarian[2] in their outlook and practical in their approach.

Raffles (1781–1826)

Thomas Stamford Raffles was born on a slave ship (his father was the Captain) in the mid Atlantic. He was forced to leave school at the age of fourteen when his father could no longer afford the fees. However, he was fortunate enough to obtain a clerical position in the East India Company in 1805, and ten years later he was on his way to Penang in northwestern Malaya to take up a position as Assistant Secretary in the Government.

[1] 此处指独立自主的
[2] 人道主义

Chapter 01

[1] 爪哇岛，印度尼西亚首都雅加达，位于爪哇岛西北部
[2] 沃伦·黑斯廷斯（1732-1818），英国殖民地官员，在印度等多地任职
[3] 授予爵位
[4] 英国国王乔治四世在1810年至1820年由于其父无法视事，被国令推举为摄政王，这段历史时期也被称为摄政时期
[5] 格子
[6] 阳台，走廊
[7] 改善

Raffles was ambitious and used his time wisely on the voyage out by learning Malay. He was soon considered fluent, and by 1811 his hard work paid off and he was appointed Governor of Java[1]. After a spell back in England and a second marriage, his first wife, Olivia, having died in 1814, he was appointed Governor of Sumatra. In 1818 he persuaded the Governor General of India, Lord Hastings[2], to agree to an expedition to set up a trading post at the southern tip of Malacca.

Although his name is forever linked with Singapore, Raffles (he dropped the "Thomas" when knighted[3] by the Prince Regent[4]) spent surprisingly little time in the trading post. However, he took a keen interest in his project, and after each visit he left clear instructions as to the layout and development of the city. He stipulated that the streets be laid out in a grid[5] pattern and that the houses conform to a specified style with a veranda[6] and covered passages to ameliorate[7] the climate. He later divided the area into *kampongs* (the Malay word for village) and promoted the education of the native Malay population. As in Java, Raffles was interested in the welfare of local people and set up wise and compassionate rules.

His life, like that of many others who lived in the tropics, including his children, was cut short prematurely. He returned to England in 1824, and two years later he died of a brain tumor. Before his death he was instrumental in the founding of the first Zoological Gardens in the world in London; he is also remembered as a great friend of William Wilberforce[1] and the antislavery movement.

Although barely remembered in the land of his birth, Sir Stamford Raffles is not forgotten in Singapore. First came a bronze statue, saved during the Japanese occupation and once again proudly on display, and then came a magnificent hotel, bearing his name, which has been a byword for luxury for many decades.

Development

British political control went hand in hand with trade and Singapore continued to flourish in the nineteenth century. In 1826 the island was combined with Penang and Malacca to form the

[1] 威廉·威尔伯福斯（1759–1833），英国政治家，英国反对奴隶贸易的领导人

Chapter 01

[1] 海峡殖民地，指1826年英国在槟城、马六甲和新加坡岛建立的殖民地
[2] 印度总督，英国在印度的管理首脑，1773年设立，1950年被废除
[3] 英国直辖殖民地
[4] 苏伊士运河，地理位置极为重要，是亚洲、非洲和欧洲往来的主要通道，连接地中海与红海
[5] 周期性地，定期地

Straits Settlements[1], ruled by the Governor of Bengal. In 1832 Singapore became the capital of the Straits Settlements; its port prospered and attracted Chinese and Indian immigrants. In 1851 the Straits Settlements became the responsibility of the Governor General of India[2]. In 1858 the administration was run directly from London through the India Office, and in 1867 the Straits Settlements became a Crown Colony[3] of the British Empire.

Economically Singapore grew from strength to strength, especially after the development of the rubber industry in Malaya and the opening of the Suez Canal[4] in 1869. Western investments, banking, and business practices brought their advantages. The end of the century saw Singapore at the hub of international trade in the region. While the Malays resented and periodically[5] rebelled against the British, Singapore remained calm and thrived as the area's primary port for the export of rubber and tin. The British authorities opened English-language primary schools, while the Chinese majority built Chinese-language

Land & People

schools.

Singapore was largely unaffected by the First World War, but after the war there was a dramatic rise in tin and rubber prices and this created great wealth for some. The strategic military importance of the island became more apparent as the British defended their colonial empire and in 1922 it became the principal British military base in East Asia. Anti-Japanese sentiment among the Chinese population grew after Japan invaded Manchuria[1] in 1931 and British officials outlawed[2] anti-Japanese demonstrations and propaganda[3].

Japanese Occupation

Japan invaded the Malay Peninsula in December 1941 and barely three months later the British surrendered Singapore. The occupation of "Syonan[4]," as the Japanese named Singapore, was brutal and savage. Thousands of expatriates[5], including women and children, were rounded up and put into camps for the duration of the War. Many never survived the starvation, disease, and cruel punishments, as was the case with many

[1] 满洲，我国东北旧称
[2] 将…驱逐出，宣告非法
[3] 宣传
[4] 新加坡1942年沦陷时被日本称为昭南岛
[5] 移居国外的人

1 声名狼藉的
2 樟宜监狱，位于新加坡东部樟宜地区，1942年新加坡被日本占领后曾被日军用来关押俘虏
3 滨海湾花园，亚洲最大的室内冷气花园之一
4 林谋盛（1909-1944），新加坡开拓者之一
5 宪兵队
6 堤道，铺道
7 西乐索炮台，位于圣淘沙西乐索海滩近山处
8 圣淘沙岛
9 蜡像馆
10 生动的场面

thousands of Allied prisoners of war. Others were tortured and imprisoned in the notorious[1] Changi jail[2]. What is often forgotten, though, is that some 50,000 Chinese men between the ages of eighteen and fifty, labeled "undesirables" by the Japanese, were arrested and summarily executed. In Esplanade Park[3] you can see the monument to Lim Bo Seng[4], a prominent Chinese businessman and resistance fighter. He was arrested by the dreaded Kempeitai[5], the Japanese Secret Police, and, despite months of torture, he refused to betray his comrades. His family also paid with their lives. Near the causeway[6] linking Singapore with Malaysia is the War Memorial to the Allied troops stationed in Southeast Asia during the Second World War who died at Fort Siloso[7] on Sentosa Island[8]. Also on the island is the Wax Works Museum[9] with tableaux[10] depicting both the fall of Singapore in 1942 and the formal surrender of Japanese forces on August 14, 1945. This momentous event ended one of the most painful periods in Singapore's history.

Many older Singaporeans, however, have

long memories and find it difficult to forget and, especially, to forgive. Like China and Korea, Singapore is still demanding that Japanese history textbooks state clearly what took place during the occupation of these countries. So far their demands have fallen on deaf ears.

Understandably the younger generation takes a more pragmatic view, realizing that the world has greatly changed in the last sixty years. They welcome Japanese investment and technology, as well as the large number of Japanese tourists who visit, spending freely in the department stores, bazaars, restaurants, and hotels.

Independence

After the War, Singapore's fortunes were inextricably[1] bound up with those of Malaya, but despite calls for a unified Malay Peninsula Britain resisted, although it became a separate Crown Colony in 1946. In the early 1950s the government of Singapore consisted of a British-appointed governor and a legislative council whose members were mostly wealthy Chinese businessmen. This

[1] 逃不掉地，解不开地

[1] 新加坡人民行动党，成立于 1954 年

introduced primary education in Singapore's four main languages. This was followed by a period in which the pressure for self-rule grew, but with student and labor unrest Britain was reluctant to cede control. However, Singapore became self-governing in 1959 with **Lee Kuan Yew** of the People's Action Party (PAP)[1] being elected as Prime Minister at the age of thirty-five. He was in favor of a federation with Malaya. Lee introduced a new flag, a new national anthem, and made English, Chinese, Malay, and Tamil the official

李光耀 (Lee Kuan Yew, 1923–2015)

李光耀是新加坡首任总理，新加坡人民行动党创始人之一，被誉为"新加坡国父"，对新加坡政治影响力巨大。李光耀有着良好的教育背景，1935 年考入莱佛士书院初中部，在日军占领新加坡后中断学业，1946 年留学英国，在伦敦经济学院学习，后转入剑桥大学学习法律，于 1949 年考获双重一等荣誉学位，取得律师资格。李光耀在 1965 年新加坡独立后积极倡导经济改革与发展，支持人才强国，主张高薪养廉和文明的生活习惯，对目前新加坡发展成为一个花园国家有着重要作用。

languages. Four years later, when Malaya gained its independence, Singapore joined the newly created Federation of Malaysia[1].

Over the decades the Chinese had worked hard, assumed managerial positions, and prospered, not only in Malaya but also in Singapore. This led to resentment by the Malays. From the beginning there were political and racial tensions in the Federation, not least of which were the concerns expressed by the Malay states that the power and influence of the largely Chinese population of Singapore would dominate the new Federation. After much agonizing and wrangling[2], Singapore was expelled[3], and on August 9, 1965, the Lion City became an independent republic. August 9 is now a National Holiday.

Lee promised to create honest government and a single multicultural national identity, and to expand trade. He fostered good relations with his neighbors so that in 1967 Singapore joined Indonesia, Malaysia, the Philippines, and Thailand in the regional Association of Southeast Asian Nations (ASEAN)[4].

[1] 马来西亚联邦，通称马来西亚。1963年马来亚联同新加坡、沙巴及沙捞越组成了马来西亚联邦。1965年8月，新加坡退出马来西亚联邦
[2] 争论，辩驳
[3] 驱逐
[4] 东南亚国家联盟，简称"东盟"。成立于1967年8月，创始国有马来西亚、印度尼西亚、泰国、新加坡和菲律宾。20世纪80年代后，文莱、越南、老挝、缅甸和柬埔寨等五国先后加入东盟，使这一组织涵盖整个东南亚地区

1 扼杀，阻止，抑制
2 使痛苦

LEE KUAN YEW

Lee Kuan Yew was born in Singapore in 1923, a third-generation descendant of immigrants from Guangdong province. He studied law at Cambridge University, England, and in 1954 he formed the People's Action Party (PAP).

It has to be said that it was Lee's personal vision, energy, and drive that made Singapore into the Asian powerhouse that it is today. Within a few years of independence the economy grew, manufacturing prospered, and the port facilities — its deep-water harbor was Singapore's only natural asset — soon rivaled those of London and New York, as it was strategically placed to be the distribution center for the rest of Asia.

Unlike many other countries in the region, the wealth from the rapid economic growth filtered down to the poorest in society. Lee was determined that obedience to the rule of law would stifle[1] corruption — something that still bedevils[2] the region. He also believed passionately in equality of opportunity, no matter what one's ethnic origins were.

Lee's vision of a prosperous, multiracial society has paid off handsomely: Singapore has a highly educated population, one of the highest literacy rates in the world, and excellent health care, social security, and transportation systems. Many citizens own their own homes in the brightly colored high-rise apartment blocks of the Housing Development Board (HDB)[1].

Although Lee Kuan Yew officially retired in 1990 to assume the post of senior minister in the Singapore cabinet, no one doubts that his influence over the ruling PAP remains.

SOCIAL CHANGE

At the time of independence the social makeup of society could be described as a Chinese majority, which, while represented in all strata[2] of society, dominated politics and government; Malays worked in the civil service, as policemen, servants, or laborers, and Indians were often shopkeepers or laborers.

Unfortunately the vision of a multiethnic society was not easy to achieve and in 1964-1965

[1] 新加坡建屋发展局，负责规划、建设及管理新建房屋的政府机构
[2] 社会阶层

[1] 逐出
[2] 煽动，挑起
[3] 吉隆坡，马来西亚首都
[4] 绝育
[5] 综合设施

prior to the expulsion[1] from the Federation of Malaysia, tension between the Chinese and the Malay underclass population boiled over. Fomented[2] by extremist groups from Kuala Lumpur[3], race riots between Malay and Chinese youths led to deaths.

Following independence, the government set out to free up the labor market by passing laws that gave employers more hiring and firing power; but workers saw changes, too, and for the first time received sick leave and unemployment benefits. Birthrates rose, and the Family Planning and Population Board began to offer clinical services, education, and incentives such as priority housing and education in exchange for voluntary sterilization[4].

The Housing Development Board

To raise living conditions and break down ethnic barriers, the new Housing Development Board (HDB) built high-rise apartment complexes[5] and relocated lower-income citizens. The complexes featured schools, shops, and recreation areas.

Land & People

Many families used their compulsory contributions to the Central Provident Fund[1] to buy apartments. Legislative support came in the form of the Land Acquisition Act[2] set up in 1967 to compulsorily acquire private land for public housing or other development programs. Together with sensitive resettlement policies, this Act enabled the HDB to clear squatters[3] and slum areas smoothly and in their place build new and comfortable HDB apartments. In the process the environment went from the squalor[4] to advanced standards. Today, about 85 percent of Singaporeans live in HDB flats compared with only 9 percent in 1960 when the HDB was first established. The government supports this public housing program by providing financial assistance for the funding of housing development and other activities. This is one of the few successful examples of the great modernist architect Le Corbusier[5]'s dream of the high-density city of the future.

The Central Development Fund

Singapore's compulsory social security savings

[1] 中央公积金
[2] 新加坡土地收购法案
[3] 住违章建筑的人
[4] 贫穷，悲惨
[5] 勒·柯布西耶（1887-1965），20世纪最著名的法国建筑师，城市规划家

[1] 免除税收的
[2] 偶然，意外事故
[3] 保健储蓄账户

scheme, the Central Provident Fund (CPF), was founded in 1955 and is an important engine of social change. Originally employees deposited a predetermined portion of their income into a taxexempt[1] account, which the employer matched. Today the rate of contribution is variable, and this adjustment is used by the government as an economic regulatory tool. The CPF is a comprehensive savings plan that has provided many working Singaporeans with a sense of security and confidence in their old age. Its overall scope and benefits encompass retirement, health care, home ownership, family protection, and asset enhancement.

CPF savings earn interest. Savings in the Ordinary Account earn a minimum interest rate of 2.5 percent per annum, while savings in the Special Savings for old age contingencies[2] and Medisave Accounts[3] earn additional interest of 1.5 percentage points above the prevailing Ordinary Account interest rate. The most significant social outcome of the CPF is that most Singaporeans are able to own their own homes.

Land & People

In the 1970s emphasis on education raised living standards, reduced poverty, and blurred class lines. Most families occupied, and many owned, HDB apartments. The command of English and technical or professional skills marked the upwardly[1] mobile.

The 1980s saw a growing need for manpower and the state responded by expanding vocational training and encouraging more women to work. An important element of this recruitment drive was the education of women. This transformed the workplace, and today Singapore is unique in Asia in terms of women's presence and position in the workforce. While this policy boosted household incomes, it had the unwelcome consequence of further lowering the birthrate, and the government launched a probirth campaign[2], offering tax rebates[3] and day care subsidies for the third child.

To ensure a balanced racial mix within HDB estates and to foster greater racial harmony, the ethnic integration policy was introduced. Even today, the HDB continues with its community builder role by working with other government

[1] 向上地
[2] 鼓励生育运动
[3] 退税

1 选区，管辖区域
2 圆形露天剧场，竞技场
3 凉亭，展示馆
4 有凝聚力的
5 非难，苛评
6 擅自穿越马路
7 破坏公共物品

ministries to provide social facilities such as community centers and neighborhood parks. Towns are planned with precinct[1] spaces such as amphitheaters[2] and pavilions[3] to give residents more opportunities to interact with one another for a more cohesive[4] community.

The 1990s were marked by the troubles in Indonesia and this led to more unskilled refugees arriving. A sign of a maturing economy was the departure of some members of Singapore's professional class for overseas opportunities.

LAW AND ORDER

The country's stability has come at a price. Many critics would argue that Singapore is over governed — a "managed democracy" with too many rules and strictures[5]. Most visitors are surprised that heavy fines are levied on those who chew gum or spit in public places, jaywalk[6], or drop litter. Smoking is banned in most restaurants and there is a heavy fine for not flushing a public lavatory after use. As for vandalism[7], it is not only punished by a fine but, in some circumstances,

the punishment is caning[1] — anything from three to eight strokes. There is no trial by jury. After independence it was initially retained for murder, but with too few convictions[2], in the view of the government, it was phased out.

In the 1980s the approach became softer and community policing was introduced and small neighborhood posts were opened. By the end of the decade 15 percent of police officers were women.

The 1990s saw the judiciary demonstrate its constitutional independence by ruling against the government in many political and civil rights cases. Although government officials intimidate political opponents and censor the press, they make no attempt to reverse rulings, or to remove or intimidate judges. Today Singapore remains a tightly ruled society, but maintains what it sees as a fair balance between openness and control.

POLITICAL LIFE

Despite the recent recession[3], the People's Action Party remains overwhelmingly[4] dominant, thanks

[1] 鞭刑
[2] 定罪
[3] 经济不景气
[4] 压倒性地

1 独裁主义的，权力主义的
2 议会候选人

both to its own popularity and to the harsh measures to limit opposition campaigning. It won eighty-four of the eighty-six seats in the 2001 general election.

The authoritarian[1] style of Lee Kuan Yew and his successor Goh Chok Tong has all but suppressed political opposition. Life is made very difficult for those who oppose the PAP; there is little political debate in the media and many parliamentary candidates[2] are returned to power without opposition. While much of this may seem oppressive to the Western visitor, it is worth remembering that for more than thirty years the PAP rule has meant wise, efficient government. The people's standard of living has steadily improved, with Singapore having the highest rate of home ownership and national savings in the world, coupled with respect for law and order. This is a multiracial society that lives in harmony.

Discussing these matters with Singaporeans is not recommended, as the government is sensitive to criticism by foreigners. Furthermore, Lee Kuan Yew and his successors feel that the West has given up on its own values — pointing to drug abuse, crime, and violence in Western society and the associated breakdown of family life and homelessness. If a Singaporean does venture any views on politics, the comment will probably be that politics is best left to the politicians, while ordinary people get on with the important business of making money.

For some young people, though, this heavily managed society can lead to problems when they leave it. There is, admittedly anecdotal[1], evidence to suggest that some of those who leave to study in the West find the unexpected and exhilarating[2] freedoms of New York, London, Sydney, or Vancouver difficult to handle.

LOW POPULATION GROWTH

Singapore's society is changing in one dramatic way, and that is in the worrying decline in the birthrate. In the period 1990–2000 the resident population growth has been only 1.8 percent per annum[3], well short of the number needed for it to replace itself. Ever since the 1980s the government

[1] 轶事的，趣闻的
[2] 令人愉快的
[3] 每年

[1] 人口统计学的
[2] 严格地
[3] 鼓励生育政策

has been aware of the demographic[1] time bomb and has rigorously[2] pursued a pro-natal policy[3], without much success.

Many women are delaying the age at which they marry and have children because they wish to pursue careers, and there are very few social services for working mothers. Lee Kuan Yew is supposed to have declared that he regretted giving women equal educational and employment opportunities in the 1960s, and the present prime minister, Goh Chok Tong, has brought in more and more incentives for women to have larger families, echoing the 1980s slogan of "go for three or more." The difference nowadays, though, is that the government pays bonuses to those who do. Of course, Singapore could again look to immigrants to keep its population growing, but as prime minister Goh recently stated,"…but they cannot replace us," as not all the new arrivals share the same cultural values and attitudes to conformity as the present population.

The government has even taken to desperate measures such as launching a "Romancing

Singapore" campaign on Valentine's Day to bring singles together by sponsoring rock-climbing trips and love-boat cruises, and setting up dating agencies so that well-educated female graduates can have the opportunity to meet prospective[1] partners.

[1] 预期的，有希望的

Chapter 02

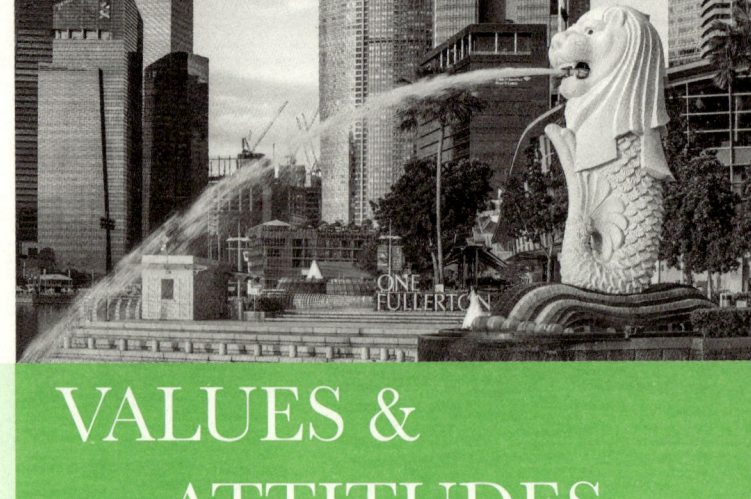

VALUES & ATTITUDES

[1] 渐渐破坏，暗地里破坏

COMMON ASIAN VALUES

The island state is home to three of Asia's great cultures: Chinese, Malay, and Indian, and although they each have their own distinct norms, values, and religions, many of these are held in common. So a Singaporean Chinese, Malay, and Indian will share much more with each other than with any Westerner. Perhaps this explains in part why Singapore has become such a successful multicultural society.

For instance, a group's or an individual's dignity is to be respected at all times, and anything that undermines[1] it is totally taboo. The "loss of face," in other words anything that severely embarrasses the group or individual, must be avoided at all costs. Furthermore all three ethnic groups, while strongly believing in equality of opportunity, also firmly believe in a hierarchical[1] society, one that gives deference[2] to age and learning, where status is earned and not simply inherited, and where position in turn brings responsibility.

Relationships are important and have to be worked at over a long period of time. Singaporeans therefore prefer to do business with people they know, such as family and friends, or school and university contacts. Thus, when there are problems, businesses first look to their suppliers and customers for help rather than to the contract and their lawyers, as is often the case in the West.

Outside a business context, Singaporeans can be synchronic[3] in their approach to time, and they consider social time commitments to be desirable rather than important. One thing at a time is not the order of the day; instead many things are done at once and time is elastic[4]. With this goes the habit of changing details and plans frequently.

[1] 等级制度的，等级体系的
[2] 顺从，尊重
[3] 限于一时的
[4] 有弹性的，可通融的

[1] 世俗的

Westerners who focus on the arrangement rather than the relationship will often find this frustrating.

Perhaps because of these values, the Singaporeans can seem indirect and ambiguous in their approach, compared to Westerners, who have a way of speaking directly and saying what is on their minds. Singaporeans do not want to upset or embarrass anyone by disagreeing, and so an affirmative answer or reply might not mean anything more than "I hear you." Similarly, Singaporeans will not usually be direct when giving bad news — they are not setting out to deceive, but they do not want to upset the hearer or damage the relationship.

RELIGION

Singapore is a secular[1] state that rightly prides itself on its religious tolerance, and its citizens are free to worship as they see fit. In fact, religion plays an important role in society and everyday life. To a great extent the different ethnic communities are defined by their religion, and many of their characteristic values, attitudes, and customs are rooted in traditional belief.

The Chinese

To the Chinese, religion is first and foremost about easing their passage through this difficult life. Their belief system is a pragmatic combination of three quite different religious philosophies — Taoism[1], Buddhism[2], and Confucianism[3]. Taken together, these address a range of spiritual, intellectual, and social needs, and have sustained the Chinese people for thousands of years.

Unsurprisingly, the Singaporean Chinese have not been influenced in the matter of religion, as they have in cuisine, by their Muslim Malay neighbors. Perhaps it had something to do with the strictures[4] against drinking alcohol and the eating of certain foods beloved by the Chinese, such as pork. Although some Chinese have converted to Christianity[5], especially the Protestant evangelical sects[6], this is an immense step for them and their families. Chinese parents and grandparents are greatly alarmed that their newly converted Christian sons and daughters and

[1] 道教，核心主张是社会人生都应以"道"及"道德"为核心，最终回归自然
[2] 佛教，世界三大宗教之一，重视人内心的修行和觉悟
[3] 儒教，儒家的核心要旨是"仁"，即修身养性、齐家治国
[4] 约束
[5] 基督教
[6] 新教福音派，不但强调维护正统信仰，更愿意关注不同方面如学术、理性和文化等的议题

[1] 尊敬，崇拜
[2] 原始的，最初的
[3] 极，极性
[4] 漩涡的，涡流的

their descendants will no longer be able to carry out funeral rites, and especially the worship and veneration[1] of the ancestors.

Taoism

Taoism is essentially about living in harmony with the natural world. The Chinese word *tao* means "way." It sees the universe as being divided into two opposing yet complementary aspects, the primal[2] forces of *Yin* and *Yang*. These polarities[3] are illustrated by the *Yin-Yang* symbol. The two swirling[4] shapes inside the circle give the impression of change — the only constant factor in the universe. One tradition states that *Yin* (or *Ying*, the dark side) represents the breath that formed the earth. *Yang* (the light side) symbolizes the breath that formed the heavens. The most common view is that *Yin* represents aspects of the feminine, being soft, cool, calm, introspective, and healing, and *Yang* the masculine[1], being hard, hot, energetic, moving, and sometimes aggressive. Another view has *Yin* representing the night and *Yang* the day. However, since nothing in nature is purely black or white, the symbol includes a small black spot in the white swirl, and a corresponding white spot in the black swirl. Each state contains the seed of its opposite.

This principle of balancing forces is embedded in Chinese thought. Everything must be in balance — in the world, the nation, and the human body — for it to prosper. According to this belief, a root cause of illness in the body is the imbalance between *Yin* (cool) and *Yang* (hot) foods. Similarly, traditional relationships must be kept harmonious, for example, between father and son, husband and wife, a ruler and his subjects, and between nation-state and nation-state. In this way Taoism, although itself an irreverent[2] and quietist philosophy, can complement the conservative[3]

[1] 男性的，阳性的
[2] 不敬的，无礼的，不逊的
[3] 保守的

1 严格
2 此处指一套
3 神
4 风水，土占
5 组合
6 门槛
7 绊倒
8 （表示）尊敬的；可敬的
9 铜锣
10 香气，焚香时的烟

rigidity[1] of Confucian teaching.

Chinese belief embraces a panoply[2] of deities[3], ghosts, and devils, and temples are sited and built strictly according to the rules of *Feng Shui*, so that they will be free from evil. *Feng Shui*, the ancient art of geomancy[4], holds that the proper alignment[5] of walls, furniture, and objects will greatly enhance the flow of *chi* — energy, or the life force — and bring prosperity to the prudent occupants of the building or the worshipers at the temple. The visitor to a Chinese temple will be aware of this as he has to step over a curb[6] that is supposed to trip up[7] evil spirits, and then pass through doors painted with images of terrifying gods and guarded by two lions, female and male, representing *Yin* and *Yang*. When stepping into the inner courtyard the visitor is obliged to remove his shoes. Although the Chinese are reverential[8] when visiting their temples, they also see them as places where the community can come together, to meet, to exchange ideas, and maybe to gossip amid the chants, gongs[9], and bells, and the perfumed smell of incense[10].

Buddhism

Buddhism addresses the problem of human suffering and finds a way to resolve it. Its founder, Siddhartha Gautama[1], the Buddha (or "Enlightened One"), was born a Hindu prince in about 563 BCE in what today is Nepal[2]. His teachings spread far beyond India to flourish and grow in China, Korea, Japan, and Southeast Asia. Born into great wealth, Siddhartha Gautama knew nothing of suffering or poverty during his childhood. At the age of twenty-nine, he renounced[3] the luxury and wealth of the palace and embarked on a quest for true knowledge. After first embracing extreme ascetic[4] practices, he reverted to[5] "the middle way" of meditation until, at the age of thirty-four, seated beneath a banyan[6], or bo, tree he experienced enlightenment.

Buddha was originally reacting against the excesses of the Brahmin[7] priests whom he had seen lusting after wealth and power, which lead to unhappiness both in this life and the next. He taught that in order to attain *nirvana*[8], or true enlightenment, one had first to recognize the

1 悉达多·乔达摩（公元前563年–公元前483年），佛教创始者，被后世尊称为释迦牟尼佛
2 尼泊尔
3 放弃
4 苦行的，修道的
5 回复，诉诸于
6 菩提树
7 婆罗门，印度种姓制度中的最高等级或僧侣阶级
8 涅槃，极乐世界。在佛教中特指阿弥陀佛的净土，阿弥陀佛的西方极乐世界

[1] 四圣谛，是佛祖释迦牟尼的苦、集、灭、道四条人生真理。四谛告诉人们人生的本质是苦，以及之所以苦的原因、消除苦的方法和达到涅槃的最终目的
[2] 佛教中的八正道，即"正见、正思维、正语、正业、正命、正精进、正念、正定。"
[3] 佛教中的三摩地，又名等持，指通向开悟的过程
[4] 上座部佛教，以八正道为根本，现主要流传于缅甸、斯里兰卡和泰国等
[5] 贬损地，轻蔑地
[6] 小乘佛教，以自我完善与解脱为要义
[7] 大乘佛教，以救助一切众生为本怀
[8] 大悲，佛教语。救人苦难之心，谓之悲；佛菩萨悲心广大，故称大悲

Four Noble Truths[1]. They are that life is suffering; there is a cause of suffering — our attachment to notions and things; there is an end to suffering — our attachment is, in essence, empty; and that the way to achieve the end of suffering is by following the Eightfold Path[2]. This depends on right thought or view, right intention, right speech, right action, right livelihood, right effort, right mindfulness, and right *samadhi*[3] or concentration.

Buddhism later split into two major schools: Theravada[4] ("teaching of the elders") — also known, pejoratively[5], as Hinayana[6] (or "lesser vehicle") — which teaches individuals how to attain personal enlightenment; and Mahayana[7] (the "greater vehicle"), which teaches the Great Compassion[8] — the practitioner delays his own *nirvana* until all other beings have been liberated. Both strands of Buddhism are present in Singapore, although the latter is more popular.

Confucian Philosophy

Not so much a religion as an ethical system,

the philosophy of Confucianism has shaped Chinese civilization for over two thousand years. The scholar-sage Confucius[1] was born in around 551BCE. He devoted his life to the study and teaching of the Chinese classics, and his writings are mainly comments on these. The origin of things lies in the union of *Yin* and *Yang*. Human relationships are hierarchical. Confucius emphasized personal virtue, promotion on merit by scholarship, devotion to the family, and justice. His precepts dealt with morality in human affairs, and continue to form a practical guide for the daily life of people. They include obedience to authority, adherence to[2] one's social position, respect for the elderly, and the veneration of ancestors. They also stress the virtues of education, hard work, thrift, loyalty, and harmony. Unlike contemporary Western value systems, Confucianism does not give overriding[3] importance to the rights of the individual; it stresses the needs of the group, and the duties and obligations of the individual.

[1] 孔子（公元前551年－公元前478年），中国古代著名思想家、教育家，开创了私人讲学的风气，是儒家学派的创始人
[2] 坚持
[3] 高于一切的，最重要的

1 使丢脸
2 （成为）孤儿的
3 无道德感的
4 不适应环境的人

CONFUCIUS' FIVE BASIC RELATIONSHIPS IN SOCIETY
Sovereign – Subject
Father – Son
Husband – Wife
Elder Brother – Younger Brother (Elder Sister – Younger Sister)
Friend – Friend

Confucianism in Practice

From infancy onward Chinese children know that they belong to a tightly knit group and they are taught never to dishonor[1] the group or bring shame upon it. If a member of the family needs help, whether it is financial or moral, the rest of the family will come to his or her aid. Taking in orphaned[2] nieces or nephews, rescuing a brother or sister from bankruptcy, and supporting a family member who is sick and unemployed are all part of family obligation. The child who places his or her needs ahead of others is considered to be amoral[3], untrustworthy, and something of a social misfit[4]!

These Confucian values, first taught in the home, are later reinforced at school, often in a practical manner — such as designating a group to be responsible for books for the whole class, or serving the rest of the children at lunch, or clearing up after lunch or at the end of the school day.

Obligation comes in many forms, but none more so than in the case of care for elderly parents. For the adult child, especially the eldest son, knows that it was his parents who gave him and his siblings the gift of life, and thereafter love and nurture. So it is the child's responsibility to attend to the needs of his parents, providing them with shelter (it used to be the norm in Singapore that three generations would live under one roof, but this is less the case now) and the wherewithal[1] to enjoy a contented old age, free from want and safe in the knowledge that after their deaths the correct mourning procedures, and the veneration due to them, would be carried out.

Education is highly valued, not only because it ensures a good career and, hopefully, a prosperous one, but because it is essential for the development of individual potential, which enhances the whole group.

Singapore is most definitely not an "I" society. How very different from Western cultures where rugged individualism[2] and self-assertiveness[3] are encouraged from an early age. Likewise, countries

[1] 必要的资金
[2] 强烈的个人主义
[3] 自作主张，专断

[1] 平等主义的
[2] 疑虑，不安
[3] 家长作风的，温和式专制主义的
[4] 利用
[5] 孝顺，孝心

in the West generally promote egalitarian[1] ideals and disapprove of status and hierarchy, although in reality we often see them in practice! Asian societies have no such qualms[2], and indeed encourage the paying of respect to people of higher status, whether it means venerating age, because of the wisdom it has brought, or learning, because of the long years of study needed to achieve a particular professional position. Similarly, the boss is looked up to in a Singaporean company and expects loyalty from his staff. In return he is expected to take a paternalistic[3] interest in their family as well as work-related problems.

The government has harnessed[4] Confucianism to create a more cohesive society, encouraging the three-tier family, filial piety[5], and education.

Young People

It is not too difficult to see that Confucian values would create a dedicated, highly motivated, and responsible workforce with an enhanced sense of commitment and loyalty. It is also true to say, however, that some young Singaporeans think that these values are no longer relevant in the modern world. In fact, the government became so concerned by this trend that it carried out a survey to find out what young Singaporeans thought were important values today. Reassuringly[1], the overwhelming majority stated that filial piety, honesty, responsibility, and self control were as important to them as they had been to their ancestors.

The Malays

Something like 99 percent of the Malay population in Singapore is Muslim. This was not always the case, as Buddhism and Hinduism[2] were the earliest religious influences, but by the time Marco Polo visited Southeast Asia in 1292, Islam[3] was well established, with mosques being built on the sites of former Buddhist and Hindu temples.

Islam

Islam was the last of the world's great religions to be founded. The word *Islam* means "entering into a condition of peace and security with God through allegiance[4] or surrender to him." The religion

[1] 安慰地，鼓励地
[2] 印度教
[3] 伊斯兰教
[4] 忠诚，忠贞

Chapter 02

[1] 先知穆罕默德（约570-632），政治家、宗教领袖，穆斯林认可的伊斯兰先知
[2] 崇拜神灵的
[3] 麦加，座落在沙特阿拉伯西部赛拉特山区，四周群山环抱，层峦起伏，景色壮丽，是伊斯兰教第一圣地
[4] 阿拉伯半岛，位于亚洲。沙特阿拉伯、卡塔尔、伊拉克等国位于阿拉伯半岛上
[5] 麦地那，位于沙特阿拉伯国境内，是伊斯兰教的第二圣地，与麦加、耶路撒冷一起被称为伊斯兰教的三大圣地
[6] 迫害
[7] 加百利，上帝为人类传递好消息的七大使者之一
[8] 伊斯兰教的《古兰经》
[9] 行动准则，规则
[10] 穆罕默德言行录，现已成为《古兰经》的一个补充
[11] （伊斯兰教的）五功，分别指念、礼、斋、保、朝。伊斯兰教规定五功是穆斯林必须履行的神圣义务，是将基本信仰付之于实践的基石
[12] 斋月，伊斯兰教历的九月

teaches the acceptance of and obedience to the word of God as finally revealed to the prophet Muhammad[1]. Born in idol-worshiping[2] Mecca[3] in the Arabian Peninsula[4] c. 570 CE, Muhammad received the call in midlife to proclaim the worship of one God (Allah) in about 616. He established the first Islamic community in Medina[5] after fleeing persecution[6] in Mecca. Today both cities are holy to Muslims.

The holy book of Islam, recording the uncorrupted word of God revealed to Muhammad by the angel Gabriel[7], is the Koran[8] (*Quran*). It contains a clear code of conduct[9] governing aspects of daily life, such as dressing modestly, and forbids the drinking of alcohol, the eating of certain foods, and gambling. The second-most important source of Islamic teaching is the Hadith[10] ("tradition"), which forms a commentary on the Koran. The fundamental duties that shape Muslim life are called the Five Pillars of the Faith[11].

It is always a good idea for the visitor to be aware of the month of Ramadan[12], the ninth month in the lunar calendar, as all good Muslims,

> **THE FIVE PILLARS OF ISLAM**
>
> **Affirmation:** the duty to recite the creed "There is no God but Allah, and Muhammad is the Messenger of God."
> **Prayer:** the duty to worship God in prayer five times each day.
> **Almsgiving:** the duty to distribute alms and to help the needy.
> **Fasting:** self-purification and the duty to keep the fast of Ramadan.
> **Pilgrimage:** the duty to make the pilgrimage, or *Hajj*, to the shrine of the Ka'aba[1] at Mecca at least once in a lifetime.

apart from the elderly, the very young, pregnant women, and nursing mothers, are expected to fast. No food or drink may be taken between sunrise and sunset. Although the fast is seen as beneficial to health, it is regarded principally as a method of spiritual self-purification[2]. By cutting oneself off from worldly comforts, even for a short time, a fasting person gains true sympathy with those who go hungry, as well as growth in his or her spiritual life. Therefore it would be the height of insensitivity[3] to eat in the presence of someone you knew to be a Muslim, whether Indian or Malay, at this time.

It is forbidden for Muslim men and women to touch members of the opposite sex outside the immediate family, so do not automatically go to shake the hand of a female colleague. Certain animals are considered unclean, so if you invite Malay friends to

[1] "天房",建于麦加的伊斯兰教寺院内的圣堂
[2] 自然净化
[3] 不敏感,感觉迟钝

[1] 口水，唾液
[2] 黑色丝绒帽
[3] 意为贤良，马来人的一种信仰

your house and you have pet dogs, it is a good idea to put them in another room for the duration of the visit. Remember a Muslim is strictly forbidden to come into contact with the nose, saliva[1], or hair of a dog.

Friday is the Muslim day of prayer, and you will see people making their way to the mosques dressed in their best clothes for the occasion. Malay men traditionally wear black velvet hats, or *songkoks*[2]. Commerce and industry accommodate Muslim devotions on Friday by arranging a specially long lunch hour from about 11:30 a.m. in the morning to 2:30 p.m. in the afternoon.

Non-Muslims are allowed to visit mosques providing they are quiet and respectful and remember to take their shoes off before entering. Visitors should be modestly dressed, and women especially should have their arms, legs, and head covered. Of course, you should always ask permission before taking any photographs. A good time to visit is between 9:00 a.m. and 12 noon, when the mosque is relatively quiet.

Budi[3]

Malays also have their own philosophical code

of behavior, which is similar in some respects to Confucianism. This is known as Budi. According to its laws the individual should always have a pleasant disposition[1], should show respect for other people, especially older people, and should always be courteous toward them. To show love and affection toward one's parents is also important, as is the maintenance of harmony in the family and society as a whole.

The Indians

The Indian community, unlike the Malay community, is not defined by one religion. Over half of its members are Hindu, but others are Muslim, others Sikh[2], while others — especially those from Southern India — are Christian.

Hinduism

Hinduism originated in North India about four thousand years ago. Superficially it embraces many apparent contradictions[3], differing forms of worship, and a profusion[4] of divinities[5]. Underlying this wide variety, however, there is unity. Hindus believe in one God: Brahman[6] the supreme,

[1] 性情
[2] （印度）锡克教徒
[3] 矛盾，抵触
[4] 丰富，大量
[5] 神
[6] 婆罗门，印度四大姓氏（婆罗门、刹帝利、吠舍和旃陀罗）之一，属于贵族

Chapter 02

1. 吠陀梵语
2. 种姓制度，世袭阶级制度
3. 雅利安人，史前时期住在伊朗和印度北部的一个民族
4. 四吠陀，又作四韦陀，古印度婆罗门教的四部圣典，包括梨俱吠陀（the rig Veda）、娑摩吠陀（the Sama Veda）、夜柔吠陀（the Yajur Veda）和阿闼吠陀（the Atharva Veda）
5. 梵文，梵语
6. 咒语
7. 印度教史诗
8. 罗摩衍那，与《摩诃婆罗多》共同为印度两大史诗
9. 摩诃婆罗多，印度古代梵文叙事诗
10. 博伽梵歌，即神之歌
11. 再生，再投胎

ultimate reality, whose many manifestations are depicted in a wealth of images. As long as a Hindu identifies himself with the Hindu faith, accepts as sacred the ancient Vedic[1] literature, and recognizes the caste system[2], he is assured a place in Hindu society.

Hinduism has several sacred works, the oldest of which are the Vedic scriptures, the tales, songs, and ceremonial instructions of the Indo-European Aryan[3] settlers in the Indian subcontinent. There are four Vedas[4] (Sanskrit[5] for "knowledge"): the *Rig Veda*, probably the oldest religious book in the world, compiled between 1500 BCE and 900 BCE; the *Sama Veda*, a collection of sacred songs; the *Yajur Veda*, the text used by priests in the performance of their religious duties; and the *Atharva Veda*, a book of incantations[6]. These, together with the great Hindu Epics[7], the *Ramayana*[8] and the *Mahabharata*[9] — the tales of early Aryan heroes, the most famous of which is the *Bhagavad Gita*[10] — contain the basic beliefs of modern Hinduism.

Hindus believe that all living beings have souls. Life is a series of rebirths and reincarnations[11] until the soul, by its virtuous behavior, is released from the cycle of birth and death. An individual's spiritual progress is determined by *karma*[1] (the law of consequence, or fate), and by *dharma*[2] (the obligation to accept one's condition and perform the duties appropriate to it). As no one can escape the duties of *dharma*, this naturally reinforces the Indian caste system. These duties are prescribed by the Hindu priest or Brahmin. Hindus therefore believe that in this life they get what they deserve; whatever happens, it is the consequence of behavior in one's previous lives. Personal duty is all-important in the Hindu faith.

The Hindu trinity[3] symbolizes the three aspects of Brahman. Brahma is the creator, Vishnu the preserver or sustainer, and Shiva the completer or destroyer. There are also many other gods and goddesses in the Hindu pantheon[4]. One of the most popular is Ganesh[5], the elephant god. He is the god of good luck, and no undertaking, apart from funerals, is contemplated without involving and making an offering to him.

[1] 因果报应，因缘
[2] 律法，守教规
[3] 印度教三大主神，分别是创造之神梵天（Brahma）、保护之神毗湿奴（Vishnu）和毁灭之神湿婆（Shiva）
[4] 印度万神殿
[5] 象头神，为印度教和印度神话中的智慧之神，是信众广泛的财神

EDUCATION

Education is highly regarded in Asian societies.

Chapter 02

[1] 精英体制

In Singapore, however, the introduction of free compulsory education has transformed the social scene. Government reforms first raised educational standards in all state schools and narrowed the gap in attainment between different social groups. Now private educational establishments are being introduced, with subsidies to keep them accessible. The universities, too, are heavily subsidized. The general high standard of education has created more opportunities for all, and this has changed attitudes. While Singapore is still in many ways a traditionally hierarchical Asian society, in the last thirty years merit has come very much to the fore, and the country prides itself on being a meritocracy[1]. English was officially designated to be the first language for the local education system in 1987. Education in Singapore features vocational education and the fundamental principle — meritocracy. Two world-top universities in Singapore are **National University of Singapore** and **Nanyang Technological University**, both of which are research universities and cover a wide range of undergraduate, postgraduate and doctoral degree programmes. In

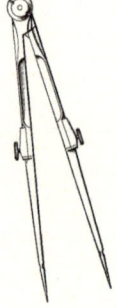

新加坡国立大学 (National University of Singapore)

新加坡首屈一指的世界级顶尖大学；在工程、生命科学及生物医学、社会科学及自然科学等领域的研究享有世界盛名。

新加坡国立大学前身为1905年成立的海峡殖民地与马来亚联邦政府医学院，1955年新加坡华人社团组建了南洋大学，1980年新加坡大学和南洋大学合并，校名定为新加坡国立大学。

根据2015年学校官网显示，该校建有三个校区：肯特岗校区、武吉知马校区和欧南园校区，设有16所学院；有教学人员2,374人，在校学生37,972人，研究生9,997人。

南洋理工大学 (Nanyang Technological University)

南洋理工大学，简称南大（NTU），是新加坡一所科研密集型大学，在许多科研领域享有世界盛名，为工科和商科并重的综合性大学。

南洋理工大学的前身为1955年由民间筹办的南洋大学，1981年，新加坡政府在南洋大学校址成立南洋理工学院，1991年南洋理工学院进行重组，更名为南洋理工大学。

根据2015年学校官网显示，该校有两个校区，其中云南校区占地200公顷，有专任教师5,546人，在校本科生和研究生33,500多人。

[1] 高等教育
[2] 意指怕输，源自闽南语
[3] 巫术，魔法
[4] （此处指）空想，纸上谈兵

addition, Singapore boasts as a "global schoolhouse" due to the fact that institutions which can offer tertiary education[1] consist of private universities, local universities and world class universities as well.

A GOAL-DRIVEN SOCIETY

A consequence of the wider opportunities now available is that younger Singaporeans of all ethnic backgrounds prize success. In the workplace this can lead to a more goal-oriented approach, rather than the traditional relationship-based dealings of their parents. Socially, perhaps, it can be seen in that uniquely Singaporean form of status anxiety known as *kiasu*[2] — literally, this means "fear of losing," or, in other words, missing out. If your neighbor is hurrying out to the shops to buy the latest piece of electronic wizardry[3], then you had better rush to do so too, in case there won't be any left. You don't want to be lagging behind. "*Kiasu*" is a word that the traveler will often hear. Because their country is so new and so prosperous, Singaporeans love to indulge in a bit of navel-gazing[4] — it is not only the visitor who wants to know what makes Singapore tick. So do they themselves.

Chapter
03

CUSTOMS & TRADITIONS

FESTIVALS AND HOLIDAYS

If you like festivals and celebrations you will love Singapore. At any given time, thanks to the many different ethnic groups, there is likely to be a festival in progress. The main events are Chinese New Year and the Hungry Ghosts festival[1], the Hindu Deepavali[2], the Festival of Lights, the Muslim Hari Raya Puasa[3], the celebration that ends the fast[4] of Ramadan, and Christmas. Some festivals are also public holidays.

[1] 中元节，俗称鬼节、七月半，农历七月的第十五天
[2] 屠妖节，也称万灯节，是印度教教徒最为看重的节日
[3] 开斋节，标志着穆斯林为期一个月的斋戒结束的日子
[4] 禁食

[1] 至，至日
[2] 一阵子
[3] 确切意义上的，严格意义上的

PUBLIC HOLIDAYS	
New Year's Day	1 January
Chinese New Year	January or February*
Hari Raya Haji	January*
Good Friday	Around April*
Labor Day	1 May
Vesak Day	April, May, or June*
Singapore National Day	9 August
Deepavali	October or November*
Hari Raya Puasa	End of Ramadan*
Christmas Day	25 December

* Dates vary according to the different lunar calendars.

Chinese New Year

The Chinese New Year, also known as the Lunar New Year, begins on the second new moon after the winter solstice[1], usually between mid January and mid February, and lasts fifteen days. Everyday life on the island seems to come to a halt for the duration. The festival is preceded by a flurry[2] of household activity: cleaning, to sweep out bad luck, cooking special regional foods of mainland China, plus shopping trips for new clothes. The celebration proper[3] starts on New Year's Eve, when

families are invited to a grand reunion dinner at the paternal home, and children pay respects to their parents. Candles burn all night and homage[1] is paid to the ancestors. The evening's activities reaffirm the family's identity and closeness. The noisy part begins at midnight, when drums and kettles are banged (firecrackers have now been banned) and windows are thrown open to usher out the old and usher in[2] the New Year.

Next morning it is the custom for children to serve their parents tea, and they in turn give them *Hong Bao*, red envelopes containing money. Family and friends visit each other over the next few days, except for the third day, which is dedicated to remembering and venerating[3] the ancestors. On the fourth day businessmen usually hold a grand banquet for their employees.

[1] 尊敬，崇敬
[2] （此处指）迎接
[3] 尊敬，崇敬

Giving *Hong Bao*

Visiting foreigners who are married should know to give *Hong Bao* to their hosts' children. Also, during the Chinese New Year a foreign manager should give *Hong Bao* to his staff. Check with your colleagues on the appropriate amount.

[1] 嘉年华般的，热闹的
[2] 妆艺大游行，新加坡农历新年的庆典活动之一
[3] 杂技演员
[4] 卫塞节，是佛教一年中最重要的一天，用以纪念佛祖诞生、成道和圆寂的日子。通常是在阳历五月份第一个月圆之日，在新加坡会通过在莲山双林寺和佛牙寺龙华院打坐、冥想来庆祝
[5] 启迪，教化
[6] 佛
[7] 红袍
[8] 经典，此处指佛经

The traditional procession marking the Chinese New Year has turned into Singapore's biggest street event. The carnival-like[1] Chingay Parade[2] features lion dances, acrobats[3], children, beauty queens, and cultural shows from different lands.

Vesak Day[4]

This day, on the full moon of the fourth lunar month of the Indian calendar, in April, May, or June, commemorates the birth and enlightenment[5] of the Buddha[6] and his entry into *nirvana*. In Singapore the various Buddhist sects celebrate Vesak Day in different ways. In the temples priests in saffron robes[7] chant *sutras*[8] while devotees pray, meditate, and make offerings. As an act of compassion, in accordance with the Buddha's teaching, captured birds and animals are set free, and alms are given to the poor. The celebration concludes with a candlelit procession through the streets.

Dragon Boat Festival[1]

The Dragon Boat Festival falls on the fifth day of the fifth lunar month, usually in May or June. It commemorates the suicide in the third century BC of Qu Yuan[2], a respected poet and loyal and honest minister of the King of Chu, who threw himself into the Mei Lo River[3] (in Hunan province) when the king refused to heed his advice. There are lively rowing competitions in Marina Bay[4] between long, thin "dragon boats" to the rhythm of drums, and these are said by some people to represent attempts to rescue Qu Yuan. Special rice dumplings wrapped in bamboo leaves called Ma Chang[5] are eaten, and again, these are said to have been intended for the fish (or in some versions, the dragon spirit) in the river, so that they would eat them and leave Qu Yuan alone. Taoist ceremonies are performed on the boats before and after the races, to bless and "awaken" them beforehand and to induce them to "repose[6]" afterward.

Hungry Ghosts Festival[7]

The Hungry Ghosts festival takes place in the

[1] 端午节，又称粽子节、龙舟节、五月节等，为每年的农历五月初五。自2008年起端午节被列为国家法定假日
[2] 屈原（公元前340年－公元前278年），战国时期楚国的辞赋家，后投汨罗江而死
[3] 汨罗江，位于湖南省，属洞庭湖水系
[4] 位于新加坡南部的滨海湾
[5] 此处指用竹叶包米制成的一种类似饺子的食物
[6] 安息，睡眠
[7] 中元节，也称鬼节，通常是农历七月半。人们在中元节有放河灯、焚纸和扫墓祭拜祖先的习俗

1 安息的
2 不吉祥的
3 营火，篝火
4 高潮

seventh Chinese lunar month, between July and August. It is thought that the restless spirits of the dead roam the earth at this time and need to be appeased[1] with gifts of food and money. This is the most inauspicious[2] time of the year. No marriages take place, children are discouraged from staying out late at night, and it is considered unlucky to buy property or close a deal at this time. The month is punctuated by dinners of many courses, *wayang* (Chinese street operas), auctions, and noisy celebrations to pacify the ghosts. Bonfires[3] can be seen all over Singapore, burning offerings of replica money — and even paper cars, houses, and mobile phones — to the spirits.

National Day

The celebration of Singapore's gaining of independence on August 9 culminates[4] in a huge parade and fireworks in the evening. All groups are represented — the ethnic communities, schoolchildren, civil organizations, and the armed forces. Each year there is a different theme, and there are weeks of practice beforehand. Tickets

Customs & Traditions

are even available for the dress rehearsal[1].

Lantern Festival[2]

Usually falling in September, the fifteenth day of the eighth Chinese lunar month, when the moon is supposed to be brighter and fuller than at any other time of the year, this is the harvest festival of ancient China, which celebrates the legend of the moon goddess, Chang-O[3]. Also known as the Mooncake Festival, it is celebrated by the eating of mooncakes — sweet pastries[4] made with flour, oil, and lotus seed — and lantern displays. At night children carry brightly colored lanterns in the shape of birds and animals in a parade. A special feature of the Lantern Festival is the dragon dance, where a huge dragon head and body, supported by a team of dancers, weaves its way around the streets collecting money on its route.

Among the legends associated with mooncakes is the overthrowing[5] of the Mongol Yuan dynasty[6] by Chinese rebels, who sent secret messages to each other hidden in the mooncakes.

[1] 排练，试演
[2] 元宵节，也称灯笼节。在新加坡，人们会经常在街上看到舞龙舞狮的场景
[3] 嫦娥，中国上古神话传说中的人物
[4] 馅饼皮
[5] 推翻，瓦解
[6] 由蒙古族建立的元朝（1271年-1368年）

[1] 屠妖节，又称光明节、万灯节，是印度教庆祝"以光明驱走黑暗，以善良战胜邪恶"的节日。在新加坡，庙宇都会点亮灯火、升起幡带，甘贝尔巷等张灯结彩的店铺会出售丰富多采的印度特色物品，以示庆祝
[2] 传说中印度的一个凶残至极的魔王，在其统治下，人民生活十分痛苦，民不聊生，后被主奎师那杀掉
[3] 主奎师那，是至尊人格首神。该名字在梵文中是黑色的意思，黑色能吸收光谱中的七种颜色，代表了他具有一切吸引力，是至极真理。主奎师那不属于物质世界，他的居所是永恒不灭的灵性世界，物质世界是其外在能量的展示
[4] 花环
[5] 拉克什米女神，象征着财富、美丽和繁荣的女神，是印度教中最重要的三位女神之一
[6] 开斋节

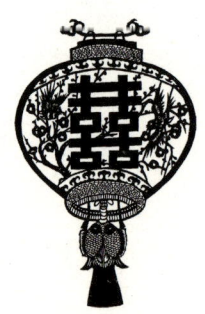

Deepavali[1]

The Festival of Lights, Deepavali or Diwali, is celebrated at the darkest time of the year, usually in October or November, and marks the start of the New Year for Hindus. The festival celebrates the defeat of the demon Narakasura[2] by Lord Krishna[3], or the triumph of light over darkness and good over evil. It is a time of rejoicing and renewal in Hindu homes. Oil lamps are lit, garlands[4] of jasmine placed at the family altar, and family and friends visit each other. Before the festival itself, houses are cleaned and new clothes bought. This is the time for the closing of accounts, for giving gifts, and offering worship to Lakshmi[5], the goddess of prosperity. Throughout Little India there is a blaze of light and sound from temples, night bazaars, and performances of traditional Indian songs and dances.

Hari Raya Puasa[6]

The date of this Muslim festival varies according to the lunar calendar, and marks the end of the month-long fast of Ramadan for Malays and

Indian Muslims. The holy month of Ramadan, the ninth month of the Islamic year, is observed with prayers and fasting during the hours of daylight. The celebration of the breaking of the fast begins with a tremendous housecleaning, the purchase of new clothes and, of course, the preparation of a splendid meal. Dishes include the seasonal *Ketupat*[1], savory rice in woven palm leaves, plus *Lontong rice rolls*[2] in banana leaves, and the ever popular *Nasi Padang*[3], which means literally "rice field" and is in fact plain boiled rice served with a selection of dishes, including curry and the famous Malay *Rending*, a dry beef or chicken curry.

The celebrations last three days. The Muslims, too, give packets of money to children when they go visiting. These are usually green in color and children naturally look forward to them.

THE CHINESE LUNAR CALENDAR

Although the visitor may see the Chinese Singaporeans as very Westernized, their lives are still governed by many traditional beliefs, including ancient Chinese *astrology*[4]. This can

[1] 马来粽，在马亚西尼、印尼和新加坡等马来族欢庆伊斯兰开斋节上常吃的食物之一，并且是开斋节的主要象征之一。用棕榈叶、槟榔叶或椰叶包裹，形状与中国的粽子相似
[2] 米饼
[3] 巴东咖喱饭
[4] 占星术，即星象学

influence important life decisions such as births and marriages.

The Chinese lunar calendar is said to have been adopted in 2698 BCE, and years are counted from then on, with some adjustments. It is a sixty-year-cycle calendar — the name of each year reappears every sixty years. Within this there are five twelve-year cycles, each year being named after one of the animals of the Chinese Zodiac[1], e.g., the Year of the Dog or the Year of the Monkey. Half the animals are domestic and half are wild, reflecting the *Yin-Yang* balance. Within the year there are twenty-four terms that mark the changes in nature and are used by farmers as a guide for planting and harvesting.

Within the sixty-year cycle, the biggest birthday celebrations are the first and the sixtieth, when the individual starts a new life. After the sixtieth year, birthdays are celebrated every ten years. Apart from the two key birthdays, people believe that the ages of 25, 29, 33, 36, and 66 are critical, and these, too, are occasions for celebration.

---

[1] 生肖十二宫，又称十二属相，包括鼠、牛、虎、兔、龙、蛇、马、羊、猴、鸡、狗、猪

BIRTHS

Chinese

The Chinese consider a baby to be one year old at birth. For the first thirty days after birth it is believed that a mother's pores[1] remain open and that cold air can enter the body. Consequently, new Chinese mothers may be forbidden to go outdoors or take a shower or bath. Diet will be high in *Yang* foods, including meat, eggs, and liver, and *Yin* foods may be avoided. Traditionally many mothers will eat specially prepared soups and broths[2] containing pigs' feet and chicken. The great celebration of the baby's birth takes place after this month and, as with all Chinese festivities[3], it centers upon food. A large number of family and friends are invited to a party, especially for a first-born child, and hard-boiled eggs with red painted shells, a universal symbol of life, are given to the guests. The guests in turn give gifts for the baby, often baby clothes in the colors of good luck — red, pink, gold, or orange, and always in matching pairs. The colors in the West that are often associated with

[1] 毛孔
[2] 肉汤
[3] 欢庆，欢宴

[1] 给予，授予
[2] 小心谨慎地
[3] 高雅人士，上层人士
[4] 占星术

babies, such as white or blue, are symbols of death in Singapore and are therefore taboo.

Malay

As with the Indian and Chinese communities, most Malay babies are born in hospitals today and many traditional Malay practices associated with the birth of a child have had to be abandoned. The child's name is formally bestowed[1] on him or her forty-four days after birth, although the name will already have been registered with the civil authorities. This religious ceremony takes place at home and is often followed by a party. There is no problem about colors of gifts for the baby, and some people like to give money, discreetly[2] enclosed in an envelope.

Indian

As with every other important aspect of life undertaken in an Indian household, a Brahmin[3] priest draws up the baby's horoscope[4] and this will be consulted at major events in the child's life. The great celebration of the birth itself takes place twenty-eight days after the child has come into the world, when its name is whispered into the baby's ear by the father. This is followed by a visit to the temple by mother and child to give thanks for a safe delivery[1] and for the baby's birth hair to be shaved off. Acceptable gifts are cuddly[2] toys and baby outfits in cheerful colors, again not white.

WEDDINGS

Chinese

Weddings are celebrated in style in Singapore. The Chinese bride dresses in the traditional white wedding dress of the West during the day, and then changes into the lucky red or pink gown for the wedding banquet in the evening. The ceremony starts with the smartly dressed groom arriving in an elaborately[3] pink and red decorated car to collect his bride. They then proceed to the groom's house where the bride is welcomed into her new family. The couple firstly honor the household gods and pay their respects to the ancestors. The all-important tea ceremony then takes place with the bride and groom offering the groom's seated parents

1 分娩
2 适合搂抱的
3 精巧地，精美地

a cup of ceremonial tea. The father, as head of the family, sips first and then his wife. In this way the bride becomes part of and is accepted by her new family. The bride is given *Hong Bao* by her new family, which may contain either money or jewelry. At this point, all the relatives are offered tea in turn according to their position in the family. After this the younger generation receives her into the family by serving her tea. The couple then move on to the bride's house where a similar tea ceremony is performed.

The wedding banquet is usually enormous, both in terms of the number of guests and the number of courses served. The bride and groom visit every table and are toasted at each. However, some couples prefer to have a wedding buffet during the day as it is less formal, usually less expensive, and guests can dance or be entertained after the meal.

Malay

A Malay wedding is equally colorful and elaborate, and usually takes place on a Saturday evening and Sunday. On the Saturday the bride waits at her home, which has been elaborately decorated with silk and satin[1] hangings[2], beaded[3] cushions, and finely embroidered throws[4]. She is the queen of the proceedings, while the groom and his family have to wait patiently in the hall or passageway outside. The *Berinai*[5], or henna application ceremony, is held prior to the wedding. The bride's palms and feet are decorated with dye from henna leaves. An official, licensed by the Muslim authorities, then speaks to the bride and groom separately, and if they agree to the marriage taking place they sign the marriage register. The groom then gives the bride a ceremonial wedding gift of about $100 and they salaam[6] each other. The couple are then legally married, but they do not start living together until after the *Bersanding*[7], or the sitting in state ceremony, the next day.

The *Bersanding* is the public celebration of the wedding and is held at the bride's home. In modern Singapore this usually means the landscaped[8] area at the entrance to the HDB[9] estate or in the enormous elevator lobby of the block where the girl lives. Marquees[10] for the guests and a sumptuously[11] decorated raised platform for the thrones[12] for the bride and groom are hired. The couple reign as King

1 缎子
2 （墙上装饰用的）帘子，帷幔
3 饰以珠的，珠状的
4 刺绣的床罩
5 指用指甲花的树叶制成的原料在手与脚上作画，象征爱情及好运的印度传统装饰艺术
6 额手礼，问安
7 在马来西亚的婚礼中公开宴请宾客的典礼
8 进行了景观美化的，进行了园林美化的
9 新加坡政府组屋。HDB是新加坡建屋发展局（Housing Development Board）的缩写
10 侯爵
11 豪华奢侈地
12 王座，君主

[1] 撒
[2] 藏红花
[3] 端正，礼貌合宜
[4] 选择
[5] 印度人结婚时最重要的婚礼金饰，在结婚当天由新郎为新娘配戴在胸前的金牌，除非离婚或丈夫不在人世才能取下这一饰物。该金牌是印度宝贵女神拉诗米（Goddess Lakshmi）的象征，在印度北部也称为"manga sutra"

and Queen over their guests and the guests sprinkle[1] rose petals and then saffron[2] rice on their palms. This ritual is to wish the happy couple a fruitful life together. In return the guests are given chocolate or a cake in a glass, symbolizing and celebrating fertility for the marriage. During this time the bride is supposed to sit with her eyes downcast and not to smile, in order to show modesty and decorum[3]. Finally, after the bride and groom step down from their thrones a traditional banquet is served.

Some couples today like to have a Western-style reception as well, usually in a hotel, for their work colleagues. For this the bride will be dressed in a Western-style wedding dress.

Indian

The Hindu wedding ceremony traditionally takes hours, but some couples opt for[4] a much simpler ceremony. The important part is when the bride and groom, watched by the priest, walk around the sacred fire that represents purity, followed by the groom's tying of the *thali*[5], a gold chain, around his bride's neck. The *thali* is the equivalent

Customs & Traditions

of the Western wedding ring, and this part of the ceremony is very noisy, with the ringing of bells and shouts and chants in order to keep evil spirits at bay[1]. Elaborately dressed guests, in saris[2] and adorned with gold jewelry, then throw yellow rice on the newly married couple and give them gifts of either money or jewelry. Even when Indian Christians marry in church, the tying of the *thali* around the bride's neck is an important part of the ceremony.

FUNERALS

Chinese

Chinese funerals are highly organized and ritualistic[3] affairs, and the ceremonies can continue for up to

[1] 使…远离
[2] 卷布,纱丽
[3] 仪式的,惯例的

Chapter 03

1. 被火化
2. 送葬者，哀悼者
3. 对尸体进行防腐处理
4. （葬礼前后的）守夜
5. 礼节
6. 刚丧失密友或亲人的人
7. 游行队伍
8. 鹳

seven days until the body is cremated[1]. The first ceremony takes place just after death, when the chief mourner[2] washes the deceased. If the death has occurred in one of the high-rise apartment blocks, the body is taken down by way of the stairs and the embalming[3] and the placing in the coffin is carried out in the open area beneath the apartment block. This is where the mourners gather; sometimes wealthy families hire extra mourners. Food and drink are provided and the mourners sit around and play mah-jong. Loud music is played to keep away evil spirits and also animals, if the gathering is outside.

If in doubt, foreigners should check with colleagues as to whether it is appropriate to attend the wake[4]. The etiquette[5] at the wake involves filing past the open coffin. You then pay your respects to the bereaved[6]. At this stage Singaporeans generally make a small gift to help with the funeral expenses.

On the day of the funeral the mourners assemble and set off in a cavalcade[7] led by a brightly colored van with the symbol of the tiger, if the person was a male, and the stork[8], if it was a woman. In China the tiger is lord of the animals. It is the emblem[1] of might and courage, and the white tiger is the guardian of graves. The stork is not only a messenger of the gods, who can carry a person to heaven, but also a symbol of virtue. The procession usually consists of family mourners followed by colorfully dressed musicians. The priest and the hearse[2] follow behind. The bereaved wear sackcloth headbands[3] and straw sandals. The body is normally cremated, in contrast to the Chinese mainland tradition, reflecting the realities of population density. After the funeral the important ritual of providing the deceased with all the material goods needed in the next life takes place. Traditionally these items were buried with the body, but today houses, cars, and mobile phones made of paper are ceremonially burned, after which the funeral party shares a large meal.

Muslim

When a Muslim dies, the Imam[4] is summoned to the house. The body is placed with the head facing Mecca, and washed by relatives, after which a

[1] 象征
[2] 灵车
[3] 粗布制的扎头带
[4] 伊玛目，穆斯林祈祷时，所有参加者必须按照伊玛目的要求完成仪式。伊玛目通常是学识渊博、有良好的道德修养及崇高威望的人

[1] 无缝合线的
[2] 清真寺

white cloth is placed over it. It is the tradition in Islam for the deceased to be buried within twelve hours of death; until then someone stays with the body with the Imam reciting prayers. Finally the body is wrapped in more layers of cloth, the last being seamless[1], and is then taken either to the mosque[2] or directly to the graveyard.

Indian

In the Indian community, when the deceased is a Hindu, the body, after washing, is placed in a wooden coffin with silver coins on the eyes to keep them closed. Two oil lamps are set on either side of the coffin, and the grandchildren process around with lighted candles. The funeral rite is conducted in the home, followed immediately by cremation. As a mark of respect for the dead person, an oil lamp remains burning in the home for as long as forty days after death.

GIFT GIVING

Generally speaking, gifts are given at weddings, Christmas, and Chinese New Year. The main point to remember for all three ethnic groups is that the present should be suitable for the occasion. It would be better not to give a gift at all than to give something cheap and tawdry[1]. Don't hand out promotional ballpoint pens or keyrings[2] to negotiating partners! Furthermore, presents should always be wrapped.

It would be considered impolite to present an unwrapped gift with the words "I'm sorry I didn't have time to wrap it." For in Singapore it is not only the thought that counts, but also how the thought is presented. An unwrapped present demonstrates your view of the recipient — he or she is not important enough for the gift to be wrapped.

It is worth remembering, not only for Singapore but also for the rest of Asia, that form is of the essence. It is not just what you do that is important, but how you do it.

Chinese

The Chinese have many superstitions[3] and you soon learn in Singapore that certain colors,

[1] 俗丽的，花哨庸俗的
[2] 钥匙圈
[3] 迷信

1 吉祥的，顺利的
2 内涵，含义
3 室内装饰
4 热带地区
5 奇数
6 广东话

numbers, and everyday items have propitious[1] or other connotations[2]. Buildings and interiors[3] should be designed according to the principles of *Feng Shui,* for example, having no sharp edges to ensure harmony.

Red, gold, and pink are the colors associated with good luck and health, fortune and happiness, while white, blue, navy blue, and black are associated with mourning. So the "Little Black Dress" is not a favorite item in a traditional Chinese woman's wardrobe, nor the white linen suit associated with life in the tropics[4] for a man.

Similarly, even numbers are looked upon favorably as everything is in a pair and harmonious, while an uneven number[5] signifies loneliness and imbalance. The exceptions to this are 4, 14, and 24, which are unlucky to many Chinese because in Cantonese[6] the number four sounds like the word "dead."

With the exception of Valentine's Day bouquets (no doubt the traditional red roses symbolize harmony, love, and good fortune), flowers are not given by the Chinese in Singapore, as they are associated with illness and death. Do not, therefore, send flowers to a new mother; and do not send a card with a stork on it, as a symbolic stork adorns a woman's funeral procession.

A gift of a clock — a favorite retirement gift in the West — would be most inappropriate, as the word "clock" in Cantonese also sounds like "go to a funeral"! Other items to be avoided include handkerchiefs, as they are *dispensed*[1] at funerals, and sharp objects, like scissors or penknives, which signify the end of a friendship.

When the Chinese give gifts, on occasions such as Chinese New Year or at weddings, they like to give *Hong Bao* — money, preferably brand-new notes, in a red envelope. If you are invited to a wedding and do not know how much to give, ask local advice. This will not be seen as a *faux pas*[2] on your part, but shows that you are sensitive to another culture and want to do, and especially be seen to do, the right thing.

In Singapore, as elsewhere in Asia, it is not the custom to unwrap a gift in front of the giver, but simply to accept it with great pleasure. In this way

[1] 分发，发放
[2] 失礼

no embarrassment is felt by either the giver or the receiver when the gift is finally unwrapped.

Malay

When giving gifts to Malays, always remember that they are Muslims — although a Chinese colleague would be delighted with a gift of brandy, a Malay would be horrified. Similarly, do not give perfume to a woman if it contains alcohol, and do not give gifts made from pigskin. If attending a wedding, a nice present would be something for the kitchen, such as a tea set, kitchen utensils[1] (but again, not knives), serving dishes, saucepans[2], and so on. The present can be wrapped in traditional wedding paper or red (for love) paper. Unlike the Chinese, people do not usually give money at Malay weddings.

Gifts are not usually given to a new mother, but if you wish to do so, a basket of fruit is always appreciated. When visiting the mother and newborn baby at home, it is traditional to bring a gift for the baby: clothing or cuddly toys, but remember — no dogs!

---

[1] 器具
[2] 平底深锅，炖锅

Indian

Like the Chinese and Malays, the Indians do not open presents in front of the giver. Unlike the Malays, the Indians believe that it is good luck to give a sum of money, if appropriate (such as for a wedding), in odd numbers[1], and this is often done by adding one dollar to a multiple of ten dollars, for example fifty-one dollars.

When an Indian baby is born, a gift of gold, such as a bracelet, is often given. Baby clothes and soft toys — again, no dogs if the family is Muslim — are also appropriate.

Although frangipani is considered beautiful and exotic by Western visitors, do not give it as a present to Indians or decorate your home or hotel room with it. It is the flower used in funeral wreaths[2] by the Indian community. Also avoid beef products or anything made of leather when giving a gift to Hindus. If giving money to a Tamil[3], the opposite rule to the Chinese applies: the notes must be given in odd numbers. If you are at all worried by this, simply seek local advice when giving a gift.

1 奇数
2 花环，花圈
3 泰米尔人

Chapter
04

THE SINGAPOREANS AT HOME

SOCIAL AND FAMILY RELATIONSHIPS

Although it is now rare to find all three generations living under the same roof, as would have been the case in some other countries, the belief in the extended family is still strong. For all three ethnic groups, the most important social unit in society is the family, and that means the extended family[1]. It is the means by which traditional values are passed on to the next generation so that one's precious cultural identity in this land of immigrants will not be lost. It is from the family that religious practice is learned, and it is from the family that the child learns to be a good Singaporean citizen. Consequently, no important decision is made

[1] （数代同堂的）大家庭

without the family's approval, whether it concerns the choice of school or university, a likely marriage partner, or business or employment decisions. Young men and women do not form attachments¹ and date if their parents do not approve of the potential girlfriend or boyfriend, and this possibly goes some way to explain why there are so few interracial² marriages. When there is an interracial marriage, the children take the father's ethnicity³.

Singapore is still largely a patriarchal⁴ society, although from its inception⁵ the government has been determined that men and women should be equal before the law and should have equal opportunities in education and employment.

¹ 喜爱之情
² 人种混合的
³ 种族地位，种族渊源
⁴ 家长制的，族长的
⁵ 起初

CHILDREN

The public displays of affection that are frowned on in Singapore do not apply to babies and young children. Indeed, it is true to say that they are overwhelmed by love, and often, to Western eyes, overindulged, for a preschooler can do no wrong. The thinking behind this is

Chapter 04

[1] 促成因素

that the real world, with all its triumphs and disappointments, does not begin until a child starts school.

Great value is placed on education, not only by the parents, who see it as improving the quality of their child's future, but also by the state, which sees it as the necessary lifeblood of the nation. A student is therefore expected to work hard at school and spend long hours doing homework. All three groups learn not only their own ethnic language but also English, and they are expected to be fluent in both. In the early years after independence many Chinese parents could not understand the reasoning behind this and argued that under British rule their children were allowed to be educated completely in Chinese, yet under their own elected government they also had to learn English. Nobody now doubts the wisdom of Lee Kuan Yew's insistence on English being taught in all schools, for not only has it been a conduit[1] to economic success, but it serves as a common language in a country that did not have one.

LIFESTYLE AND HOUSING

The really wealthy live in palatial[1] houses on "landed property." Affluent[2] Singaporeans live in large, luxurious private apartments complete with swimming pools and squash courts[3]. They are very much in the minority. About 85 percent of all families live in high-rise HDB apartments that they are either buying or aiming to buy. The apartments are well furnished and contain all the latest electronic and technical gadgets.

INVITATIONS HOME

Gifts

It is always appreciated if the visitor brings a gift, but remember the Malays and Indian Muslims do not drink alcohol and frown upon smoking, so sweets or cakes are a good idea. If your hosts are Chinese, remember to keep to even numbers, except 4, 14, and 24, which are unlucky.

Etiquette

It is a great and rare privilege to be invited to a

[1] 富丽堂皇的
[2] 富裕的，有钱的
[3] 壁球场

Chapter 04

1. 从一边的，向旁边的
2. 把…塞进，把…藏入
3. 初学走路的孩子

Singaporean home, and so as not to give offense here are some points to be aware of. In all three communities it is the custom to remove your shoes when entering the home (so wear socks or tights). Remember to dress modestly. It is probably better to dress more formally than you might normally dress if visiting Western friends — so no shorts or revealing clothes, even if it is hot and humid outside.

In Malay homes you may well be invited to sit on the floor, and here you have to be careful not to point the soles of your feet at anyone, so if you are a man sit cross legged and if you are a woman, sitting sideways[1] with your feet tucked[2] under you usually solves the problem. If, however, you are invited to sit on a sofa or a chair, it is a good idea not to cross your legs, especially in front of an older person, as this is regarded as rude. Where children are concerned, in the West it is usual to pat a small child or toddler[3] on the head, but in the Malay and Indian world the head is considered to be sacred and should never be touched. Above all, do not use the left hand when eating, shaking hands, or giving gifts in Malay or Indian households, as it is reserved for personal hygiene[1] and considered unclean.

In all three communities it is the tradition to offer some refreshment, however brief the visit, and it would be impolite to refuse. If you are invited to a meal in the evening, remember that Singaporeans tend to rise early and retire early, so take your cue[2] from your hosts. Unlike in the West, guests may not stay on after the meal but leave promptly when it is finished.

Public and Private Areas

Singaporeans have definite public and private areas, and the visitor can cause grave embarrassment if in conversation he unwittingly[3] touches on close personal or family relationships, emotions, romantic attachments, or sexual matters. Displays of affection are frowned upon and the Western habit of hugging and kissing close personal friends of the opposite sex is not even considered. Similarly, discussions about religion or the political environment are best avoided, and

[1] 卫生
[2] 提示，暗示
[3] 不经意地，无意地

[1] 自贬的，谦虚的
[2] 此处指紧紧的，用力的
[3] 紧握
[4] 伸开的，延伸的

humor does not always travel well — especially British humor, which is often self-deprecating[1].

GREETINGS

Chinese people will often shake hands, but it is not the firm, vigorous[2] grip[3] of North America or Northern Europe, but rather a softer and more gentle gesture. You will also probably see an older Chinese man pat a younger friend on the arm as a way of greeting.

When greeting each other, Malays will probably salaam, that is, put their palms together and make a small bow. They might use the other traditional Malay greeting of offering both hands to the recipient, lightly touching the person's outstretched[4] hands, then bringing one or two hands back to the heart. Your hosts, knowing you are Western and wanting you to feel at home, may very well shake your hand, but again, Malay women do not expect to shake hands with a man and a Malay man would not generally expect to shake hands with a Western woman. Unlike countries in continental Europe and South

America, Singaporeans do not go in for hugging or kissing, even with close friends.

Similarly, in the Indian community different sexes do not shake hands with one another, although an Indian woman will shake hands with another woman and a man with another man. The traditional Indian greeting of *namaste*[1] is similar to that of the Malay salaam.

PUBLIC DISPLAY

All the communities respect age because of the wisdom it brings and expect dignified behavior in front of an older person. They all feel uncomfortable with public displays of affection, and with touching members of the opposite sex, so a handshake may not be an appropriate greeting. It is a good idea to maintain a reasonable social distance, about an arm's length, away from the opposite sex. This is slightly further away than most Westerners are familiar with. A friendly smile and nod of acknowledgment[2] gets around any difficulty. In contrast, Singaporeans of the same sex touch freely and hold hands as signs of

[1] 印度的合十礼,即双手合并放置在心脏的位置,闭上双眼低头
[2] 感谢

[1] 求爱，求婚
[2] 协调的，一致的
[3] 媒人

friendship and closeness, nothing more.

BOY MEETS GIRL

Interracial marriages are rare as cultural influences are so strong. Dating and courtship[1] within the three communities of Singapore is a relatively new phenomenon. Marriage was considered far too important a matter to be left to casual dating and romance — it was seen as the final step into adult life and responsibility, necessary for the creation of the next generation. Romantic love was considered a bonus in marriage and not obligatory, and most marriages were arranged by parents who considered that they knew and understood their children better than they did themselves. The parents would try to find a partner from a similar background, whose personality would be compatible[2], thereby ensuring as far as possible that the marriage would be harmonious.

In the past, and on occasion even now, especially if the young person is shy and reserved, Singaporean families would use a matchmaker[3] to find the ideal partner for their child. In this

The Singaporeans at Home

way they would ensure that religious, social, and educational criteria were properly considered, and, in the case of an Indian betrothal[1], that caste laws were strictly adhered to. Horoscopes[2] for both Chinese and Indian families would be studied carefully, as would the background of the prospective bride or groom, and if anything untoward[3] were found, the marriage would definitely not go ahead.

Today young people in all three communities are encouraged to get to know each other as friends and to have a social life of dinners, outings, and parties as part of a group. In conservative Singaporean families, individual dating as known in the West, where a boy or girl has many dates, is frowned upon, and indeed this kind of behavior could jeopardize[4] their marriage prospects. So young people get to know each other at school, university, and in the various social clubs attached to their places of employment.

Dating below the age of seventeen is also disapproved of, as parents feel their children should spend their time on their all-important studies and

[1] 婚约，订婚礼
[2] 星占，算命天宫图
[3] 麻烦的，不幸的
[4] 危害

[1] 前兆
[2] 订婚
[3] （构成整体）的一个组成部分

preserve their good reputations. Thereafter, when a boy and girl decide that they like each other, and more importantly if the parents approve of the prospective partner, they will start going out together as a couple. This is usually the precursor[1] to marriage, and so it is important that a Western visitor realizes exactly what dating means in Singapore. If by any chance the boy or girl's family feels unhappy with the dating arrangements, then the young people will take note of their wishes not to proceed. In the Indian community dating does not start until after the engagement[2] has taken place.

NATIONAL SERVICE

At the age of sixteen and a half, every Singaporean male has to do two to two-and-a-half years' national service, and later reserve duty until the age of forty. This is a useful opportunity for the different strands[3] of society to mix and work together. The experience of being thrown together with people from different backgrounds for a common purpose creates social ties and fosters a shared sense of identity. Position and promotion in the army depends on performance. The government may choose to defer[1] national service for target groups to suit the social and economic needs of the moment, but no one is exempt.

NAMES

In Singapore the three ethnic groups refer to themselves in very different ways and because this is still a formal society it is important to get personal names and titles correct. If ever in doubt, seek local advice for it will show that you are sensitive to the issue.

The correct forms of address in Singapore can be complicated. Generally, when making introductions and in formal meetings it is advisable to use a person's title first and then their family or personal name, for example "Vice President Lee." Titles are usually used for superiors, but not for equals or juniors. Although many younger Singaporeans adopt a Western-style personal name, such as Lucy or Brian Wong, for everyday use, most elder Singaporeans do not, and it is

[1] 推迟，延期

[1] 犯错
[2] 充满…的
[3] 惊人的发现
[4] 优先

always better to err[1] on the side of formality rather than give offense.

Chinese

Chinese conventions can be fraught with[2] difficulties for the Western visitors, and something of a revelation[3] when you work out the system.

Given the importance of family to the Chinese, it comes as no surprise that the family name is given precedence[4] in the order of an individual's names. For example, if a man's family name is Wong he would be called "Mr. Wong." Mr. Wong probably has two given names, so he might be Wong Chok Yew. This is where it gets slightly complicated, because the name Chok will have been given to all the sons of that generation in the family. Finally, he will have his personal name, Yew. Therefore Mr. Wong's full name is presented, from the general to the particular, as Wong Chok Yew.

When being formal it is a good idea to address somebody as Mr., Miss, or Madam, followed by the family name, for example "Miss Lee." Friends call each other by their given names. In business, take your cue from your counterpart.

Chinese women, on the other hand, traditionally retain their own (paternal) family name on marriage as they are obviously not of the bloodline[1] of the husband. So Mr. Wong's wife is technically not Mrs. Wong, although she might be known by her Western friends by this name. If her maiden name was Lee Bee Wah, in which Lee was the paternal family name, it remained the same when she married and she became Mrs. Lee. Sometimes Chinese women changed their name by joining it with that of their husband — in this case she would have been Mrs. Lee-Wong Bee Wah. Occasionally the honorific[2] title of Madam was used, as in Madam Mao Tse Tung or Madam Chang Kai Shek.

In Singapore, Chinese women tend to use their husband's name. If they want to retain their own name, they use their maiden name plus "Madam."

Chinese women, like the men, will often adopt a Western personal name, especially if working for a foreign company, so Lee Bee Wah might refer to herself as "Betty."

[1] 血统
[2] 敬称的，表示敬意的

Chapter 04

[1] 困惑的
[2] 叫卖的小贩
[3] 此处指女孩

If all this seems a little too complicated, just ask people what they would like to be called. And remember, Chinese people are equally bemused[1] by Western names, especially if a person's name is Robert and suddenly they hear him being referred to as Bob, or Alexandra as Sandra. Tell your Chinese friends and colleagues what you want to be called from the beginning so that you avoid the embarrassing situation of being referred to in the office as Mr. Robert or Miss Alexandra.

In Singapore, children refer to older people who are not related — parents' friends, shopkeepers, salesmen, hawkers[2] — as "Auntie" or "Uncle." Foreigners are sometimes bemused to hear the term used in unlikely circumstances.

Malay

Malay men attach their father's name to the end of their own name and use the word *bin*, which means "son of." So, for example, Ali bin Osman is Ali, son of Osman.

Similarly women use *binti*[3], or "daughter of." So Fatima binti Osman is Fatima, daughter of

Osman. Her friends will call her Fatima and in more formal terms she will be addressed as *Puan* (Mrs.) Fatima or Mrs. Fatima. As with the Chinese and Indian communities, some Malay married women (especially those in business) will adopt their husband's name in the Western manner. If you see the word *Hajji*[1] or the feminine *Hajjiah* in a person's name, it means that he or she has undertaken the pilgrimage[2] to Mecca.

Indian

The forebears[3] of the majority of the Indians in Singapore came from Tamil Nadu[4], where they do not use family names. Instead they use the initial of their father's name placed before their own personal name. For example, a woman named Radhika would call herself M. Radhika, where M is the first letter of the name of her father, Murugesan. After marriage, Radhika will be addressed as Mrs. Radhika, followed by her husband's personal name or both his names.

Not all Indians in Singapore are Hindu or Muslim — some are Sikh and others Christian.

[1] 男性伊斯兰教徒，女性使用 Hajjiah
[2] 朝圣之旅
[3] 祖先, 祖宗
[4] 泰米尔纳德邦，位于印度南部

Chapter 04

[1] 宗族，部落
[2] 分支
[3] 辛格，姓氏。

Unlike the Chinese, if you hear an Indian refer to himself by his Christian name, such as Thomas or Patrick, then he will indeed be a Christian, and this is not just a Western name he has adopted for ease of pronunciation.

Most Sikhs have three names: a personal name, a name to show Sikh identity ("Singh" or "lion" for a male), and a clan[1] or sub-sect[2] name. Many Sikh names are the same as, or similar to, Hindu ones. All Sikhs are Singhs[3], but not all Singhs are Sikhs. (Singh, meaning lion, is included in the name of Singapore!) Men are often addressed as "Sardarji" (abbreviated to S.), which is an honorific similar to "Mr." Most personal names can be used for both males and females. Women often just use "Kaur" (meaning "princess") as a third name, but can also use "Singh" as many families have taken this as a surname.

Chapter 05

FOOD & DRINK

Food plays an important role in the social life of Singaporeans. The blending[1] and adapting of the Chinese, Malay, and Indian culinary[2] traditions has resulted in a distinctive[3] new cuisine. Typical Singapore dishes range from the classic Chili Crab, Hokkien Prawn Noodle soup[4], and *Murtabak*[5] (stuffed Indian bread), to more recent introductions such as Stingray[6] in Banana Leaf (from Malaysia), and tea-smoked Sea Bass[7]. Smoking food over a mixture of tea leaves is popular in Yunnan and Sichuan provinces of China, but there it is usually done with duck.

The fusion[8] of these strong traditions began in Singapore's earliest days. Indeed, it could be said

1 融合
2 饮食的，烹调的
3 有特色的
4 福建虾面汤
5 卷饼
6 黄貂鱼，也称赤魟，体型较大属食用鱼类和观赏鱼
7 此处指鲈鱼，海鲈鱼
8 熔合

Chapter 05

1. 汇聚
2. 主食
3. 空心菜
4. 调味品，调料
5. 马来式米粉，又称暹罗米粉
6. 喀拉拉，位于印度的西南端，渔业极为发达
7. 此处指鱼鳃下的肌肉部分
8. 多汁的，多水分的

that the modern fashionable idea of "fusion food" first started in Singapore.

Due to the huge influx[1] of Chinese migrants, Malay food soon incorporated such Chinese staples[2] as bean sprouts, soy sauce, noodles, and bean curd. Spicy *Kangkung*[3] is a good example of a dish where both Malay and Chinese seasonings[4] are used to bring out the flavor of the leafy green vegetable *kangkung*. Straits Chinese from Malaysia combine Nonya cuisine with the Chinese love of pork, which, of course, is forbidden to Malay Muslims. Similarly, Chinese noodles are often served in a spicy coconut broth, as in *Mee Siam*[5]. Again, this is a firm favorite in Nonya cuisine, but not seen in mainland China.

If Chili Crab is Singapore's national dish, Fish Head Curry is not far behind. This was a recipe invented fifty years ago by a young chef, originally from Kerala[6]. This dish is not seen in his native South India, but to the Chinese the head of the fish, and especially the cheek pocket[7], is the most succulent[8] and delicate part. Matched with a curry sauce, it soon became a firm favorite and today there are many variations and interpretations of this curry.

The local Indian population has also produced an Indian variation of Indonesian *Mee Goreng*[1] — fried wheat noodles with chilies, potato, and bean sprouts — served with a spicy curry sauce. One way in which the Chinese will eat mutton is in the hearty North Indian Mutton Soup. It is always a popular dish in the food stands as it makes a great lunch or late night supper dish. The soup is enlivened[2] with lots of fresh coriander[3] as well as other dried spices and, to give it a new twist, it is served with crunchy French bread. *Murtabak*, a classic Indian Muslim dish consisting of bread stuffed with minced meat and onion, is very popular.

Chilies, which are essential in Indian cooking but not in Chinese, apart from the northern provinces of Sichuan and Hunan, appear in nearly every Singaporean Chinese noodle or rice dish. Indeed, it would be hard to imagine these dishes without them.

More surprising, though, is the fact that

[1] 印度炒面
[2] 使有生气，使活跃
[3] 芫荽，是香菜的学名

[1] 印度甜调味料的一种
[2] 辣酱油，又称"喼汁"，一种起源于印度的地方调料
[3] 红酒烩牛肉
[4] 高良姜，山柰
[5] 鸡汤饭
[6] 此处指用蔬菜包裹的烤鱼
[7] 此处指猪肉干

Singaporeans have also been influenced by the food of their former colonial masters. Fruit chutneys[1], tomato ketchup, Worcestershire sauce[2], and more recently balsamic vinegar, have all been a source of inspiration, as well as potatoes and slow-oven baking. A vaguely English oxtail stew[3] was often cooked by Hainanese cooks in colonial homes, and this has now been interpreted in a Malay/Indonesian style as Sour Hot Oxtail Stew, or *Buntut Asam Pedas*.

Indonesian cuisine is represented in the widespread use of fragrant spices such as galangal[4], a root similar in appearance to ginger. As the ancestors of many Malay Singaporeans came from Java, a firm favorite is the Javanese Spicy Chicken Soup with Noodles, or *Soto Ayam*[5]. Braised Fish in Pickled Vegetables, or *Acar Ikan*[6], is another traditional Malay/Indonesian dish. Satays[7] are also very popular but, unlike in Indonesian and Malaysian cuisine, in Singapore they have been adapted to Chinese tastes, and are therefore often made with pork.

COOKING STYLES

Barbecuing and grilling[1], long used by cooks in Malaysia, soon joined Chinese stir-frying, braising[2], and steaming techniques. Different provinces of China — depending on the climate and cooking fuel available — developed different culinary styles, and it is true to say that all of these are in use in Singapore. Although the Cantonese community is relatively small, this is not reflected in the many Cantonese restaurants and in the widespread enjoyment of *Dim Sum*, a popular Hong Kong lunchtime dish. Hokkien food is strong on pork, which Indian and Malay Muslims are forbidden to eat, but the Hokkien *mee* — the yellow wheat noodles — are popular with everyone. Indeed, they have been incorporated into Malay dishes such as *Mee Rebus* or *Soto Mee* and the Indian/Indonesian *Mee Goreng*.

Teochew[3] food relies heavily on fish. Indeed, the men of Teochew in Southern China were traditionally fishermen. The Teochew fish ball, like the Hokkien *mee*, is accepted by all creeds[4]. In fact the Chinese, being the good businesspeople they

1. 烧烤
2. 炖，焖
3. 此处指潮洲的
4. 教义，信条

[1] 伊斯兰教律法规定的合法食物

are, have gone further than this and established *Halal*[1] (food prepared according to Muslim dietary laws) Chinese restaurants where their Muslim neighbors can comfortably eat, safe in the knowledge that they are not breaking any of their food laws.

DIETARY RESTRICTIONS

The Chinese, apart from Buddhists in the South of China who do not eat beef, have no restrictions on what they can or cannot eat — perhaps because of a history of years of famine and desperate poverty, everything is fair game. Indeed, the Chinese greeting is not "Hello" or "How are you?" but "Have you eaten?" The reply, incidentally, is always "Yes," even if you haven't.

However, that does not mean to say that all Singaporean Chinese like the same food: mutton and lamb are highly prized in the north of China but heartily disliked everywhere else, largely because of the smell, and this applies to the Singaporeans who come from South China. Dark chicken meat to the Chinese is the delicacy, not the white. In general they dislike large slabs[1] of meat, and especially underdone meat such as rare steak. In China people from the north like noodles, steamed bread, and dumplings because the climate is too severe to grow rice; whereas rice is popular in the more wet and humid south. In Singapore both rice and noodles are popular.

Although the Chinese love to eat, they eat with health very much in mind. They believe that certain foods are "*Yin*," or "cooling." Foods such as pork, watermelon, and apples cool the body down and are good in summer. "*Yang*" foods on the other hand are considered to be hearty: fried foods, chocolate, and lychees[2] are examples that fit into this category. You are guaranteed a healthy diet by balancing *Yin* and *Yang* foods. In other words: everything in moderation.

Malay and Indian Muslims are forbidden certain foods, with pork being at the top of the list. All other meats and poultry have to be slaughtered[3] according to strict *Halal* rules.

[1] 厚的切片
[2] 荔枝
[3] 宰杀，屠宰

1 沿街叫卖者
2 重新安置
3 活跃的，熙攘的
4 冒气的
5 极热的
6 高档的

FOOD COURTS

Hawkers[1] once roamed the streets of Singapore selling all kinds of tasty foods. Now they have been relocated[2] to permanent centers, but the tasty snacks have not changed.

These open-air hawker centers are not for quiet, elegant dining. They are bustling[3], noisy places, full of smells coming from steaming[4] pots and sizzling[5] pans, with orders being frequently shouted to the cooks. Many Singaporeans regularly eat out at such venues and all have their favorite places. They represent excellent value for the money and there are those who swear that the meals in such places are just as good as, if not better than, meals served in many upscale[6] restaurants. Certainly these are the places to enjoy the best *Mee Goreng*, *Wan Tan Mee* (noodles served with stuffed dumplings), and *Char Kway Tiao* (stir-fried rice noodles).

In the shopping malls, air-conditioned food courts serve hawker food, but in greater comfort.

DRINK

Chinese tea is the normal accompaniment[1] to a meal. The Chinese believe that it prevents obesity[2] by washing away the fats ingested[3] with the food, and when taken after a meal it helps digestion. They do not drink coffee after meals. Furthermore, they like to drink one or two glasses of Chinese tea before a banquet, where there are going to be many alcoholic toasts.

As a general rule, the Chinese do not like drinking without eating and therefore dislike cocktail parties. They will drink beer with their meal, usually the splendid local Singapore brew "Tiger Beer," and, surprisingly, given their dislike of iced drinks, they drink it cold. They also like drinking brandy — the more expensive the better, as it is seen as a status symbol. For Indian and Malay Muslims alcohol is strictly forbidden.

This section would not be complete without mentioning the legendary Long Bar of the Raffles Hotel, source of Singapore's most celebrated cocktail, the Singapore Sling[4].

[1] 伴随物，此处指同食的东西
[2] 肥胖
[3] 可吸收的
[4] 新加坡司令，著名的鸡尾酒

[1] 一种甜酒
[2] 酸橙

SINGAPORE SLING

Original Recipe

2 parts Gin

1 part Cherry Brandy

1 part Benedictine[1]

1 part Triple Sec

2 parts Pineapple Juice

2 parts Orange Juice

1 part Lime[2] Juice

Quick and Simple Recipe

3 parts Gin

1 part Cherry Brandy

Juice of 1 Lemon

In both recipes mix and strain into a tall glass, top with soda water, and decorate with sliced orange, lemon or lime, and a cherry.

Chapter 06

TIME OUT

TOURISM

Singapore, given the convenience of its Changi airport[1] hub[2] and the pains of jet lag[3] for the intercontinental traveler, has set out to attract the stopover visitor. It actively promotes the comfort of a few days in one of its luxurious hotels, with the opportunity to taste its appealing mix of cultures in the dramatic modern city, or to unwind[4] and enjoy the peace of a timeless backwater idyll[5].

  Shopping in a tax-free city flowing with international fashion designer labels gives the satisfying sense of getting a bargain that appeals to shoppers, however many dollars they have in their pockets.

[1] 新加坡樟宜机场，是新加坡主要的民用机场和亚洲重要的航空枢纽
[2] 中心
[3] 时差
[4] 此处指放松
[5] 此处指不受外界干扰的田园式生活

[1] 大众快速交通，也称地铁或捷运
[2] 解说

Tourism contributes about 5 percent to Singapore's GDP and is strongly promoted by the government. The reputation for being a safe destination with superb hotels continues to attract millions of visitors each year. However, in 2003 the number fell from around 7.5 million per annum of the last few years to just over 6 million, almost all due to the SARS virus that reduced travel to most Asian countries. Nevertheless Singapore continues to receive regional awards for tourism, whether for the private individual, the businessman, or the convention visitor.

GETTING AROUND

Transportation in and around Singapore, whether by taxi, bus, or Mass Rapid Transit (MRT)[1], is easy and relatively cheap. A good way to see the sights and get an idea of the geography is to take a guided cruise of the Singapore River with a commentary[2].

MRT

The MRT is one of the most efficient underground

rail networks in the world. Trains run everyday from 5:30 a.m. until midnight. They are clean, air-conditioned, and, best of all, outside the city center of Singapore the tracks run overground. Remember to keep some small change not only for the MRT ticket but also for the buses. A souvenir card with a stored value of $5.50 in fares is available for $6.00, the $0.50 being a premium[1] as you keep the ticket as a souvenir.

Buses and Trams

The bus network is far more comprehensive than the MRT, and slightly cheaper. Buses are also air-conditioned and operate daily from 6:00 a.m. until midnight. There is a tourist bus that covers most of the sights and runs daily from 9:00 a.m. to 6:00 p.m. Another good way to sightsee is to take a tram[2] called the Singapore Trolley[3], which travels along the Orchard Road[4], the old colonial area, the Singapore River, and passes Raffles Hotel. You can purchase a ticket either from your hotel or the driver and this will entitle[5] you to unlimited journeys and a riverboat tour.

[1] 额外的费用
[2] 有轨电车
[3] 电车
[4] 乌节路，新加坡著名的商业旅游街
[5] 使享有权利；使符合资格

[1] 招呼，招呼致意
[2] 安装计价器的
[3] 拥堵费
[4] 追加罚款
[5] 东方快车，五星级标准的列车
[6] 丹戎巴葛火车总站
[7] 桂河，新加坡著名的旅游景点

Taxis

Taxis are plentiful on the streets of Singapore and you can hail[1] them or pick them up at designated stands. Fares are reasonable, and every taxi has them clearly displayed. All cabs are metered[2] and tipping is not expected. Remember though that if you are traveling in the city center — known as the Restricted Zone — you will have to pay a congestion charge[3]; there is a surcharge[4] at peak period times, and also after midnight.

Singaporean taxi drivers may not always speak English very well, and it is worth having your destination written down in English.

Trains

Regular train services run between Singapore and key cities and towns on the west coast of Malaysia. For a really luxurious trip, try the Eastern and Oriental Express[5]. It departs from Tanjong Pagar Railway Station[6] and takes in the sights of Penang and the River Kwai[7].

Rickshaws[1]

In Singapore you can also hire a rickshaw, or "trishaw[2]" as it is known locally. This is a three-wheeled bicycle with a carriage on the back. Today these are only a tourist attraction, not a regular form of transportation. Remember to negotiate the price before you commence your journey.

Car Rental

On the other hand, there is no negotiating the cost of renting a car. Rentals are high, parking is expensive, and the government has introduced disincentives[3] in order to combat traffic congestion. The only benefit of a car would be if you were planning to continue your trip into Malaysia.

    Driving is on the left and, of course, if you drive into the Restricted Zone in the center of the city there is a charge to pay. The speed limit is 30 miles (50 km) an hour, and 50 miles (80 km) on an expressway. Driving under the influence of drugs or alcohol is dealt with severely.

[1] 黄包车，人力车
[2] 脚踏三轮车
[3] （此处指使人受挫的）措施

[1] 延迟地，延续地
[2] 令人激动的；使人动感情的
[3] 修理
[4] 恢复，修整
[5] 刺激性的

DESTINATIONS

Chinatown

The first Chinese immigrants, who arrived in 1819, were allocated an area south of the Singapore River to settle in by Sir Stamford Raffles. Soon thousands of others arrived, largely from the central and southern Chinese coastal provinces, and Chinatown became a lively trading settlement. This is remained until the 1970s, when the government started to replace the old buildings with modern HDB apartments. Belatedly[1] it was realized that this threatened the loss of yet another atmospheric[2] part of old Singapore, and the city architects began a program of renovation[3] and restoration[4], so that some of the old shops selling paper goods to burn at funerals, teas and teapots, red paper lanterns, Chinese books, and traditional clothing have been retained.

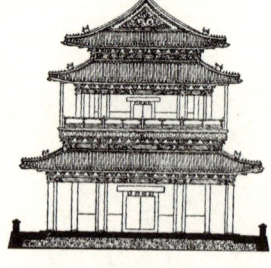

Here you get a feeling of what Singapore must have been like in the early 1900s — bustling streets, noisy with the sound of different dialects, filled with the pungent[5] scents of food cooking, and thronged[1] with people. Many of the shop houses were two or three stories high, depending on the family's affluence. Sadly some have had to be demolished[2] in recent years due to the construction of the MRT that has led to new stations at Clarke Quay[3] and Chinatown, but at least this makes it easy for the traveler to visit the area.

The best way to explore Chinatown is on foot, giving yourself at least three or four hours. Not only is there a lot to see, but the weather is hot and humid and can be debilitating[4] if you are not used to it. Take along plenty of sunscreen and a good pair of sunglasses, and wear a broad-brimmed[5] hat.

Arab Street

The area north of the Singapore River and west of the Rochor River[6] was designated a Muslim settlement by Raffles and soon attracted Arab traders. Today it still reflects the traditions of those Arab seafarers[7], Indonesians, and Malays who came to settle here. The shops of Arab

[1] 挤满的
[2] 被毁坏的，被破坏的
[3] 克拉码头，新加坡市区最新的娱乐场所
[4] 使人衰弱的
[5] 宽边的
[6] 梧槽河，源头在武吉知马，位于新加坡加冷
[7] 船员

Chapter 06

1 蜡染的布
2 藤制品
3 篓编织品
4 苏丹回教堂，新加坡最大最为壮观的宗教建筑，可同时容纳五千名教徒做礼拜。回教堂内禁止穿鞋，是新加坡古迹
5 圆屋顶
6 尖塔

Street are a blaze of color, selling cloth of all kinds, including silks and batik[1], rugs, brassware, gold, and jewelry, as well as rattan ware[2] and basketry[3] that overflow onto the sidewalk. The air is filled with the marvelous smells coming from the many Halal restaurants, especially around the Sultan Mosque[4].

The first mosque was built on the island in 1826 thanks to a generous grant from the East India Company. One hundred years later, the Islamic community had outgrown this and the Sultan Mosque was built. This is now the city's principal mosque. It can accommodate five thousand worshipers and has a golden dome[5], towers, and minarets[6]. Visits are strictly regulated and the best time to come is during the month of

Ramadan — when the sun sets and Muslims can break their fast, the surrounding streets are full of enticing[1] food stands.

The name Arab Street[2] applies not only to the street itself but to the whole area bounded by Rochor Canal Road, Jalan Sultan, Victoria Street, and Beach Road. The easiest way to get there is to take the MRT to Bugis[3].

Little India

Little India, surprisingly considering the history of Chinatown and Arab Street, was not designated as an ethnic quarter, but simply grew of its own volition[4] in the latter half of the nineteenth century. It is largely concentrated north of the Rochor Canal and is easy to get to — simply take the MRT and alight[5] at Little India station. The main artery[6], Seragoon Road, stretches[7] a mile from Rochor Canal Road to Lavender Street, and can easily be explored on foot. Brace yourself for a sensory[8] experience — there is so much to see, delicious foods to smell and sample, and wonderful items to buy.

[1] 吸引人的
[2] 阿拉伯街，独具特色的商业街，著名的苏丹回教堂位于此街。是优质丝绸、藤制品、蜡染、香水等的集中地
[3] 武吉士，地铁站名。位于新加坡中心地带，是著名的购物、美食和社交场所
[4] 决心，意志力
[5] 此处指下车
[6] 干线，要道
[7] 延伸
[8] 感官的

1 拱廊
2 香料

There are goldsmiths selling jewelry created from ancient Indian patterns. The Little India Arcade¹, a cluster of shops from the colonial era, sells sari fabrics — some with gold and silver threads woven into them. Visitors sometimes buy lengths of sari material for use as exotic bed hangings back home, or as elaborate table runners. The nearby "Spice² Route" shop is worth visiting to see or, perhaps more importantly, to smell the ground mixed spices. The brightly packaged spices make unusual gifts, and they come with the added bonus of easy-to-make recipes.

All this can easily take a good half day, and Sundays are best avoided unless you like crowds. Sunday is the day when migrant workers from all over South Asia come here to chat, eat, worship, and shop, and at times it can seem as if the entire subcontinent has gathered here!

Historic Singapore

At the heart of the old colonial settlement is the Padang ("field" in Malay), a large, well-tended[1] open space surrounded by trees that was earmarked[2] by Raffles as a recreation ground soon after his arrival. Here are the grand colonial buildings that are still used for the city's administration. Many were designed by the Irish architect George Coleman[3], and if you later wander up to the first fort on the island, Fort Canning, you can see his gravestone together with those of other early settlers. It is a sobering[4] exercise to read the inscriptions on these headstones as so many of the first British arrivals died in their twenties, killed not by war but by tropical diseases. The hill itself, in addition to containing the ruins of the fort, is landscaped with shrubs and trees.

[1] 受到精心照料的
[2] 被标记的
[3] 乔治·科尔曼(1795–1844), 爱尔兰著名建筑师
[4] 使严肃的，使冷静的

[1] 代表，表现
[2] 约瑟夫·康拉德（1857-1924），出生在波兰，30岁时开始学习英语，后成为著名的用非母语写作的小说家
[3] 拉迪亚德·吉卜林（1865-1936），英国著名小说家、诗人，出生于印度，代表作有《丛林故事》等
[4] 萨默塞特·毛姆（1874-1965），英国著名小说家、戏剧家，其代表作《月亮和六便士》描写的是一个英国画家来到南太平洋后与土著人共同生活的故事
[5] 艾娃·加德纳（1922-1990），美国著名女演员
[6] 伊丽莎白·泰勒（1932-2011），著名好莱坞女演员

Raffles Hotel

A visit to Singapore would not be complete without a visit to the legendary Raffles Hotel. Since opening its doors in 1887 it has epitomized[1] colonial elegance, luxury, and style, and given rise to an exotic cocktail — the Singapore Sling. Writers such as Joseph Conrad[2], Rudyard Kipling[3], and Somerset Maugham[4] stayed here, as did glamorous Hollywood movie stars like Ava Gardner[5] and Elizabeth Taylor[6].

Chinese Garden

For those interested in gardening or in search of a few peaceful hours' relaxation, a trip to the Chinese Garden and the nearby Japanese Garden, at any time other than the weekend, is very worthwhile. Both are close to the MRT Chinese Garden station to the west of the city.

Sentosa

This tiny island, immediately south of Singapore, was formerly a British military base. It is now a favorite resort for locals and tourists alike. One of the main attractions is the Underwater World[1], the largest oceanarium[2] in Asia. A moving walkway[3] through two huge tanks allows you to view exotic fish such as giant rays and thick-lipped garoupa[4] close up. If your visit coincides with one of the many feeding times, it can be even more exciting. It is a good idea to check the times beforehand.

The colorful Butterfly Park[5] with some 2,500 specimens is also worth visiting, and of course, this being Singapore, there are the beautiful but inevitable orchid gardens.

If you fancy being a little less active, a visit to the southwestern coast of the island will take you to sparkling beaches created from specially imported sand, coconut palms, and flowering shrubs.

The Smaller St. John's[6] and Pulau Ubin Islands[7]

For the more adventurous, there is also St. John's Island, just under four miles (six km.) south of Singapore, which is less developed than Sentosa. There are no hotels there, but there are some

[1] 海底世界
[2] 海洋水族馆
[3] 走道
[4] 石斑鱼，多栖居于热带及温带海洋，肉质洁白，营养丰富
[5] 蝴蝶公园，有约120余种蝴蝶和100余种植物，有马来西亚典型的雨林环境
[6] 圣约翰岛，曾为监狱，现成为著名的旅游景点
[7] 乌敏岛，位于新加坡东北部，主要由花岗岩组成，因此开采花岗岩是岛内主要的经济活动

Chapter 06

1. 平房
2. 礁湖，咸水湖
3. 高跷捕鱼小屋
4. 红树林
5. 舨船

magnificent former colonial bungalows[1] to rent. You can swim in the lagoons[2], picnic in certain designated spots, and watch a wide variety of bird life, some of which has made a successful bid for freedom from the bird sellers on the main island. It takes about an hour to get to St. John's and the ferries leave from the World Trade Center. Check with your hotel for the times of sailings.

If you really want to step back in time to see the Singapore of fifty years ago, visit the island of Pulau Ubin, about one and a half miles (two km.) off the northeastern corner of Singapore. You can simply sit looking out to sea, admire the traditional Malay stilt fishing huts[3], or visit one of the Taoist or Buddhist temples on the island. The more energetic can rent mountain bikes to explore the forests and the mangrove[4] swamps that abound with wildlife. Details of these activities can be obtained from the visitor center near the ferry. Bumboats[5] leave from Changi Point once there are enough people on board.

Malaysia and Indonesia

Regular ferry services also operate between Singapore and the Malaysian resort island of Tioman¹, as well as the nearby Indonesian islands of Batam² and Bintan³.

RULES AND REGULATIONS

Visa

For a stay of up to thirty days a visa is not required for visitors with passports issued by North and South American and European countries, excluding former member states of the USSR⁴. Travelers with passports from other countries should check with the Singapore government Web site (www.gov.sg) or the local Singapore consulate⁵ for visa requirements. In all cases six months' validity⁶ on your passport is required. In addition, travelers should have round-trip tickets and sufficient funds for their stay in Singapore.

Drugs

Trafficking⁷ in all but the smallest quantity of

1. 刁曼岛，位于马来西亚东部，由64个小岛组成的火山群岛之中最大的一个，是新加坡人喜爱的旅游去处之一
2. 巴丹岛，是印尼距新加坡最近的一个岛屿
3. 民丹岛，是印尼寥内群岛的最大岛屿，由于位置接近赤道，因此终年阳光普照，是高尔夫球爱好者的好去处
4. 是 the Union of Soviet Socialist Republics 的缩写，指前苏联
5. 领事
6. 有效期
7. 非法交易

[1] （此处指）毒品
[2] 招致，带来

narcotics[1] is punishable by death on conviction.

Driving

A valid driver's license from your own country or a valid international driver's license is required for driving in Singapore.

Fines

Singapore has been dubbed "Fine City." Smoking is not permitted in public service vehicles, museums, libraries, elevators, theaters, cinemas, air-conditioned restaurants, hair salons, supermarkets, department stores, and government offices. There are tough fines for offenders. Other civil offenses that incur[2] fines include jaywalking, littering, urinating in an elevator, not flushing a public toilet, and chewing gum!

MONEY

There is no restriction on the amount of currency you can bring in, and major credit and charge cards are widely accepted.

The local currency is Singapore dollars and

cents. U.S. dollars and British pounds are also accepted in most major shopping centers and big department stores.

Banking hours are Monday to Friday, 10:00 a.m. to 3:00 p.m.; Saturday, 9:30 a.m. to 1:00 p.m. (some banks are open until 3:00 p.m.); and Sunday, 9:30 a.m. to 3:00 p.m. (some banks in Orchard Road).

Most banks handle traveler's checks and change foreign currency. Passports are required when cashing traveler's checks. A commission may be charged.

Apart from banks and hotels, money can be changed wherever the sign "licensed money changer[1]" is displayed, which applies to most shopping complexes. Visitors are discouraged from changing money with unlicensed money changers.

SAFETY

Singapore's reputation as a safe and secure destination is well known, and it enjoys one of the lowest crime rates in the world.

---

[1] （此处指）换零钱的地方

[1] 肉豆蔻香料

SHOPPING

Of course, no visit to Singapore would be complete without a shopping trip or two, or three, and one of these expeditions must include a visit to Orchard Road. This legendary street got its name from the many nutmeg[1] and pepper plantations that lined the streets until the early years of the twentieth century, when a mysterious disease totally wiped them out. How very different Orchard Road looks today: here you will be spoiled for choice. Large department stores, shopping malls, and exclusive boutiques offer a range of international products as well as Asian artifacts, furniture, Persian carpets, jewelry, table linen, silks, batiks, and the latest electronic goods. Despite the heat and humidity, you can shop in comfort, as the malls and shops are all air-conditioned and many of them are interlinked. However, if you are interested in bargains and lower prices in general, hop on to the efficient MRT to one of the suburbs and experience shopping like the locals. Nearly every housing estate has its shopping center with a variety of shops, from the humble corner store to elegant designer label shops.

The Great Singapore Sale

The Great Singapore sale takes place in the run up[1] to National Day. Every shop in Singapore has a month of sales, usually in June or July. To pick up a designer label at a bargain price, go to stores that sell last season's stock or overruns[2] at discount prices. Your hotel and the local newspaper are the places to ask and look for what's available and where. You could possibly do the same at the leading department stores such as Robinsons[3] or Tangs[4].

    The latter is a perfect example of a Chinese rags-to-riches[5] story. Over forty years ago, a former lace peddler, C. K. Tang, had the foresight[6] to see that the site now opposite the Orchard MRT Station would become a bustling thoroughfare[7]. He subsequently brought building materials from his home in Swatow[8] in China and started constructing a department store. In 1982 the site was redeveloped and now contains not only a department store but also a high-rise hotel.

[1] 事件的前奏
[2] （此处指）过多的货物
[3] 罗敏申百货公司，新加坡著名的百货公司
[4] 诗加董百货公司
[5] 白手起家的，从贫穷到富裕的
[6] 远见
[7] 通路，大道
[8] 汕头

¹ 符合条件的，合格的
² 有背胶的标签

However, it was rebuilt in the traditional Chinese style, with a green roof and red pillars, and Tangs is recognized today as a leading home-grown department store selling the best of local fashion and design.

Sales Tax

Most shops levy a 5 percent Goods and Services Tax (GST), but the good news is that you may be eligible[1] for a refund when you leave Singapore if your purchases exceed $300 and if you get the shop to complete the necessary documentation. Look out for the Tax Free Shopping sticker[2].

Shopping Hours

Shops are usually open from 10:00 or 11:00 a.m. until 9:00 or 10:00 p.m., and are open on public holidays as well. So there is no excuse not to "shop till you drop."

NIGHTLIFE

Singapore does not spring to life after dark as, say, Bangkok or Hong Kong do. Bars and nightclubs exist, but anyone in search of racier[1] forms of nightlife is likely to be disappointed. One of Singapore's most famous night sights used to be Bugis Street[2], where gorgeous transvestites[3] would promenade[4] and noisy bars would stay open until the early hours, but the area disappeared in 1985 when it was bulldozed[5] to make way for the MRT. However, in true Singapore style, a sanitized[6] version of Bugis Street has been re-created, with closed-circuit TV and plainclothes police to ensure that soliciting does not occur. Where there are transvestites, these have been hired as "customer relations officers" to explain the history of the area to the visiting public.

Nightclubs are increasing in number and quality, however, in response to the growing demands of young and relatively wealthy Singaporeans, as well as the expatriate community and tourists. Cover charges are fairly expensive and the dress code is conservative smart casual.

1   （此处指）色情的
2   武吉士街，是新加坡规模最大的平民购物街
3   异性装扮癖者
4   散步，漫步
5   （此处指）被拆除
6   （此处指）整装一新的

1 不变的，固定的
2 户外的，露天的

Most clubs will close around midnight during the week, although as you would expect they stay open until the early hours on the weekend.

Bars not only have a more relaxed dress code, but have extended happy hours, which certainly helps the visitor on a tight budget, as alcoholic drinks are expensive. In order to counter its rather staid[1] reputation, Singapore recently lifted the ban on bar top dancing and now allows pubs to stay open all night.

Boat Quay and Clarke Quay on the Singapore River are both lively places full of restaurants and bars where alfresco[2] dining is popular. In the middle of the nineteenth century, Boat Quay was

the center of the Singapore River's commercial life, but a hundred years later the area had fallen on hard times. The government, realizing that it was in danger of over-sanitizing Singapore, decided to restore some of its historical charm. The façades[1] were retained and restored, and new eating places and watering holes quickly opened up. Harry's Bar on Boat Quay has become famous, or perhaps infamous, as the bar where Nick Leeson, the trader who brought down Barings Bank, used to hang out. It offers food and live jazz, available in equal measure.

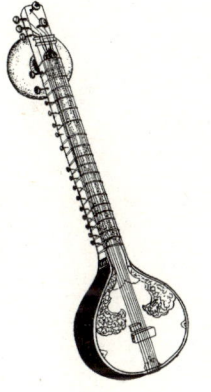

Further up the river is Clarke Quay. Again, this has been renovated, but it has a different atmosphere from Boat Quay, being more geared to families. On Sunday there is a lively flea market here.

CULTURE

All the various ethnic groups in Singapore have formed cultural societies to maintain and sustain their identities, and here music and dance play important roles. The playing of the *sitar*[2], the

[1] 外观
[2] 西塔尔琴，一种木制长颈的印度拨奏弦鸣乐器

[1] 合唱曲
[2] 中途停留
[3] 新加坡榴莲艺术中心，也称滨海艺术中心，是特色鲜明的艺术表演场地。外型犹如两颗大的榴莲，是最具特色的现代建筑之一

classical Indian stringed instrument, the staging of colorful operas from Canton, Hokkien, and Teochew, and the magical sound of the Malay *gamelan*, a native version of the Indonesian ensemble[1] of gong and chimes, all contribute to a vibrant cultural life. Every June there is month-long Festival of Arts. In addition there is an annual film festival and regular productions of live theater.

Furthermore, because of its colonial background, Western ballet and classical music have a large local following, and the city is a regular stopping-off[2] point for performing arts companies touring East and Southeast Asia. It is easy to dip your toe into the varied waters of Singapore's cultural life. You can find out what is going on in the English-language newspapers (look in the *Straits Times)* or at your hotel, which will help to arrange the tickets.

Well worth visiting are the Singapore Art Museum, particularly for its outstanding collection of contemporary Asian art, the National Museum, and the Esplanade[3], a huge new integrated arts complex on the waterfront east of the Padang, home to the Theaters on the Bay, (popularly known as the Durians[1], after the fruit, because of their shape). This bold project reflects the government's drive to foster a unified Singaporean culture.

[1] 榴莲

Chapter
07

BANQUETS & ENTERTAINING

All business as well as most social entertaining is done in restaurants. Banquets are a feature of Chinese business life and the celebration of major family events. Guests often arrive late so as not to appear greedy and, since Singapore is a hierarchical society, they often arrive in order of rank. The banquet will usually take place in a private dining room in a hotel or restaurant.

EATING ETIQUETTE

The solitary diner is a rare sight in Singapore. Eating is a communal event in all ethnic groups, although the manner of dining differs. For the Malays, Indians, and Straits Chinese, eating with your fingers is the only true way to enjoy curry. However, only the right hand is used because, among traditional Hindus and Muslims, the left hand is reserved for personal hygiene. Even then only the tips of the fingers of the right hand are used, and it is considered most impolite to touch another person's food with your fingers. When helping yourself from a communal[1] dish, always use the serving spoon provided. Diners wash their hands before the meal, and you may find yourself being offered a bowl of warm water and a napkin both before and after a meal in finer Indian or Malay restaurants. Even in the most basic of establishments you will often see a row of wash basins provided for the use of their customers.

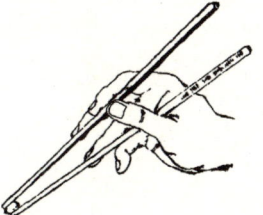

For the Chinese, dining etiquette is somewhat different as the use of chopsticks is the norm. There are certain straightforward[2] rules governing their use. For instance, never put your chopsticks upright in a bowl of rice as it symbolizes death. It is also considered to be bad manners to wave your chopsticks about, point them at somebody, or make a noise with them (although it is more than

[1] 公共的
[2] （此处指）明确的

Chapter 07

[1] 出声地吃
[2] （此处指）筷子托
[3] （食物）大小适合入口的
[4] 份量

acceptable to drink soup noisily or slurp[1] noodles). It is permissible, from time to time, to rest one's chopsticks on the rest stand[2], never across the dinner plate or rice bowl. It is bad manners to reach across another person's chopsticks in order to get at the food on display.

Unlike the West, guests do not stay long chatting and drinking coffee after the end of the meal. When everyone has finished eating, that really is the end of the festivities and usually all the guests leave at the same time.

For the Malays, forks and spoons will usually be provided for a meal, but not knives as these are considered to be weapons. However, do not worry as any meat will already have been cut up into bite-sized[3] portions. The fork is held in the left hand and used to push the food on to the spoon. It is considered impolite to make a noise with a spoon when serving yourself, and you should always ask your host to join you in eating. The Malays are delighted if you take second helpings[4] and, unlike the Chinese, do not think you are being greedy, so you do not have to protest when

Banquets & Entertaining

offered more, but graciously[1] accept. On the other hand, it is considered rude to refuse food, so at least try to sample a small piece when served. If you absolutely cannot eat the food proffered[2] you should invent a good excuse, such as an allergy.

SEATING ARRANGEMENTS

Typically the table will be round with a revolving central platform for the dishes, so the whole group can see, speak to each other, and help themselves to food without interruption. The place of honor, unlike in the West, is on the left side of the host. The more junior guests sit with their backs to the front entrance. This comes from the time when it was feared that armed assailants[3] could burst into a room and attack those nearest the door first. However relaxed the evening is, there will always be a seating plan, and so one waits to be seated. Of course, the host does not take his seat until everyone else has taken theirs.

So as not to be seen to be bragging about[4] the evening's fare, the host will probably say a few words about the paucity[5] and insignificance of the

1 亲切地，殷勤地
2 提供，提议
3 攻击者；行凶者
4 吹嘘
5 少数，少量

[1] 社交礼节上需要的
[2] 祝酒辞
[3] 放慢速度

food on offer. The guests respond to this humble stance by admiring the food as it appears, discussing with fellow guests the subtle flavoring and composition of each dish. Usually a banquet consists of eight or ten courses and the dishes appear one at a time. The use of chopsticks is *de rigueur*[1] at an event like this, but in the home many Chinese use forks, spoons, and plates.

MAKING SPEECHES AND PROPOSING TOASTS[2]

In order not to spoil the enjoyment of the food, all speeches are made before the banquet begins. To commence the proceedings the host will raise his glass and propose a toast, or simply say "*Ch'ing.*" The other guests similarly raise their glasses, holding the glass in both hands, the fingers of the right hand under its bottom, the left hand holding it. There can be further toasts throughout the meal when each new course appears.

It is a good idea to pace yourself[3] at a banquet, or you risk being overwhelmed by the time the last dish appears. You are not obliged to eat a lot of any food you do not like, but you should eat whatever you serve yourself. Always take the food from the dish nearest to you on the revolving circular[1] table top.

RECIPROCATING[2]

It is part of doing business in Singapore to be entertained and to entertain in return, and even though your own country might be far less formal, Singaporeans will usually feel more comfortable if entertained "Singapore style." Whether the "return match" is at home or in Singapore, the same basic rules apply.

First, the hotel or restaurant chosen should be of sufficiently high standing and reputation to impress your guests. Second, the function will need to be held in a private dining room. When considering the menu, it is a good idea to establish whether any of your guests are Singaporean Malays or Indians as the menu will need to reflect this. Muslims do not eat pork or drink alcohol and Indians are often vegetarian[3].

If you are entertaining in Singapore take

[1] 能旋转的圆形用餐桌
[2] 互惠的
[3] 素食者

[1] 尽管，虽然
[2] 用屏风隔开

local advice as to the suitability of the venue, the menu, and the number of courses that would be appropriate. It is important to get help with the seating plan — and name place cards, with correct spellings and title, of course — in this hierarchical society. The Western practice of "sit anywhere" causes great confusion and embarrassment. You as the host will need to be there in plenty of time, not only to greet your guests but also to check that everything is in order.

Arranging this in your home territory might prove a little more difficult. It is always sensible to play it safe and entertain in a Chinese restaurant, albeit[1] one of excellent standing. Singaporeans will feel at home in such a place, and if any of the team is Malay or Indian, the restaurant will be able to provide suitable vegetarian dishes. Chinese restaurants in the West are, of course, familiar with private dining rooms, and will nearly always have one or be prepared to screen off[2] part of the restaurant for the visiting party. You might wish to dine in the chosen restaurant beforehand to see if it and the service are up to the mark, and then later spend some time talking to the management about your requirements for the meal. A careful and methodical[1] approach pays handsome dividends, as your guests will realize that you have gone to a lot of trouble on their behalf and will be suitably impressed.

How Not to Do It

The senior managers of a Western company inadvertently[2] entertained their Singaporean colleagues in the worst possible way. The hosts chose a very prestigious[3] hotel with a splendid private dining room, but after this things went from bad to worse.

First, they had drinks before dinner, not realizing that Singaporeans feel distinctly unhappy drinking without food, and do not like to eat too late either.

The menu was chosen with care, but with no thought as to the requirements of their guests. The main course was rare roast beef[4]. Singaporean Chinese do not like eating large pieces of meat, let alone eating it rare, and as for the Malays and

[1] 有方法的，有系统的
[2] 不注意地
[3] 声望很高的
[4] 三成熟的烤牛肉

[1] 以同样的方式
[2] 失礼，失言
[3] 破坏，崩溃

Indians, it was a disaster.

Dessert followed in the same vein[1]. Singaporeans always have fresh fruit sliced into small portions, but on this occasion a large chocolate pudding was served. This was far too rich for the guests, and as for the cheese course that followed, Singaporeans as a rule dislike dairy products.

The meal finished with coffee, and each guest was given a present of an unwrapped ball point pen with the logo of the host company.

The entire occasion was an example of how not to entertain Singaporeans. Fortunately, despite the *faux pas*[2], the business relationship did not founder[3], and eventually after a more appropriate meal, a deal beneficial to both parties was signed!

Chapter 08

BUSINESS BRIEFING

THE ECONOMIC MIRACLE

The initial business advantage of the island came from its location on the shortest route for ships between the Indian Ocean and China and Japan. This coupled with free-trade colonialism[1] and an influx of immigrants liberated from the constraints of their homelands gave the country an environment for economic growth.

[1] 殖民主义

When Singapore became independent it was a small territory with no natural resources, and a poor, unskilled workforce. Lee Kuan

1 （此处指）激励措施
2 双位数的
3 经受得住，安全渡过
4 关税保护

Yew and Finance Minister Goh Keng Swee set out a development strategy with the state as principal investor in an export-oriented free-market system.

However, within a few short years, Britain announced its withdrawal from the military base that contributed 20 percent to the island's GDP. This was a massive blow, but in some ways it was a blessing in disguise as it forced Singapore to stand on its own two feet and to seek competitive advantage by converting the old British naval base into the world's third-largest commercial port.

The island's manufacturing and industrial base was expanded by attracting technologically strong foreign companies with various tax incentives[1]. The government controlled industrial financing and development, and invested heavily in education. The result in the late 1960s was double-digit[2] GDP growth.

In the early 1970s government policies to expand trade and industry and attract foreign investment paid off. Singapore managed to ride out[3] the 1973 oil crisis with slower but, nonetheless, single-digit growth. Tariff protection[4] for the electrical and electronic sectors was reduced and financial services became a focus for growth. By 1975, Singapore was the world's third-largest oil-refining¹ location and its third-busiest port, and five years later it became Asia's most important financial center after Tokyo and Hong Kong. The government then targeted computer technology and electronics as the next phase in Singapore's industrial development.

Singapore weathered² the 1997 Asian financial crisis, but its export dependence caused a recession in 2001-2012. Competition from other countries spurs³ the government to seek trade alliances and economic restructuring. Today the U.S.A. remains its single largest trading partner, followed by Malaysia, Hong Kong, and Japan.

Singapore's success since independence has rested on its recognition that it needs to retain a regional competitive advantage against countries in the region. It has sought to do this by adapting its work and management styles and by investing in education, skills, and technology. This has been reinforced by the ease of entry for foreign

¹ 炼油
² 受到冲击
³ 鼓励,给予刺激

[1] 东盟自由贸易区，于1992年倡议提出，现包含原来的东盟六国（印尼、马来西亚、菲律宾、新加坡、泰国、文莱）及四个新的成员国（越南、老挝、缅甸、柬埔寨），旨在促进贸易流通，发展经济
[2] 废止，废除
[3] 业已决定的
[4] 预算盈余
[5] 贬值

investment in a corruption-free stable economy. Singapore is also pressing for an ASEAN Free Trade Zone[1] and seeking to create bilateral free-trade arrangements with Australia, Canada, Japan, and the United States.

FINANCIAL MANAGEMENT

Initially the Singapore government tied its currency to the U.S. dollar but by the late 1970s the currency had been floated and all controls on currency exchange abolished[2].

Singapore's compulsory Central Provident Fund, founded in 1955, deposits a predetermined[3] portion of worker income into a tax-exempt account, which the employer matches. The Fund, which covers worker retirement and disability, also creates consistent budget surpluses[4] and a national savings rate of nearly 50 percent of GDP.

The 1997 Asian financial crisis inflated Singapore's prime lending rate to nearly 8 percent and devalued[5] its dollar slightly against the U.S. dollar. Debt-free status helped Singapore recover quickly. The lending rate soon fell back to 6 percent, and huge foreign reserves — the world's largest in per capita[1] terms — cushion[2] the dollar.

In the last few years the devaluation of other Asian currencies has eroded[3] Singapore's competitiveness. With virtually no official controls on the movement of capital, Singapore cannot use monetary policy to stimulate or suppress its economic activity. The government has consequently opted to cut business costs by reducing employer contributions to the Central Provident Fund rather than attempt to devalue the currency.

Singapore trades in shares, bonds, derivatives[4], and commodities twenty-four hours a day and so overlaps with the trading hours in both the U.S.A. and Europe. The financial institutions range from insurance to investment banking to providing services targeted at the expatriate community.

It is all too easy in commerce and industry for the visitor to be seduced[5] by the Western dress, behavior, and excellent English of those around you to think you are in a Western country and

1 每人，照人数分配的
2 （此处指）缓冲
3 腐蚀，破坏
4 衍生债券
5 诱惑，吸引

revert to your home behavior. You should not! When doing business in Singapore it is vital to be aware of what is considered acceptable conduct.

BUILDING RELATIONSHIPS

Time is needed to build a Singaporean business relationship, as it is founded on trust and mutual respect. Once established, it is worth its weight in gold. Do not plunge into business when first beginning a meeting. Singaporeans, like other Asians, prefer to get to know the person they are dealing with; after all, he or she is the personal face of the company at the moment. Take time to show them that you are a reliable person. Business relationships are based on honor and integrity. Take the trouble not only to establish contacts but to maintain them. Trusted networking or *guanxi* has been the main way of getting anything done in China and Singapore for decades. Although *guanxi* is usually based on family, school, and university ties, because of the obligation that members owe each other, non-Singaporeans can enter this "magic circle" if they are able to demonstrate that they are trustworthy, and this in turn can open up trading networks in Singapore and further afield[1] in Southeast Asia.

Finally the important thing to remember about business relationships is that they must be nurtured with both direct and indirect contact. A failure to do so will expose your business to attack from competitors.

INTRODUCTIONS

People in Singapore do not look directly into the eyes of the person they are meeting as this is a sign of disrespect. This can be disconcerting[2] when you first experience it and it is certainly not a sign of shiftiness[3]!

The normal verbal exchange on introduction is to express pleasure at meeting. If business enters the conversation in any way the discussion should be modest. Do not talk up[4] your business.

When introducing people the etiquette is always to mention higher before lower rank, older before younger, and a woman before a man (unlike the rest of Asia, except for Hong Kong).

[1] 在远处，在远方
[2] 使人窘迫的
[3] 狡猾
[4] 说清楚，直说

[1] 主动
[2] 气氛，氛围，格调

The handshake is the normal business introduction between members of the same sex but not between opposite sexes. If a woman wishes to shake hands with a man she must make the move[1], and only do it on introduction. The handshake should be soft and linger a while. Crushing bones and vigorously shaking the arm of the other person is not done!

It is important not to draw conclusions from how a person looks at you or shakes your hand when you first meet, as the etiquette is totally different from that in the West.

SMALL TALK

Good topics of polite conversation are positive things about Singapore, including how well it is developing, how wonderful the food is, how attractive the scenery, how you are enjoying your stay. Always start meetings, even if you know the person, with five minutes of general discussion before plunging into the agenda. To do otherwise is to set the wrong tone[2] for the discussions ahead.

Bad topics are anything critical of Singapore

or its government, or anything about sex, religion, and politics.

HANDS

Within the Chinese community items such as gifts, including *Hong Bao* money and business cards, are given and accepted with two hands. With Malays and Indians never use the left hand for handling food, money, gifts, shaking hands, giving business cards, or any other transaction.

When using your right hand, remember not to point at a person; rather use the whole of the right hand, palm upward, in a gesturing motion. When ordering a taxi, simply turn the palm down, beckoning[1] toward yourself.

BUSINESS CARDS

Because the Singapore business environment is so hierarchical it is important to note a person's position in a company. For this reason business cards are crucial. When you receive them you will notice that one side is written in English and the other in Chinese. Take a minute or two to study

[1] 向…示意，召唤

[1] 夸张的，夸大的
[2] 准时

them; not only is this being courteous to the giver but, importantly, it lets you know the position and authority of that person in their company. Have your card printed in both Chinese and English and take local advice as to the most appropriate title to put on it. This is necessary to ensure that you get to meet the right people in the company you are visiting. Even though you might be a little embarrassed at your high-sounding[1] title, it has been recommended for a good reason.

When handing out business cards, you should give them to everyone present, using both hands, with the print facing the recipient so that it can be read easily. Never put a card in your back pocket or write on someone's business card. Both actions will give offense.

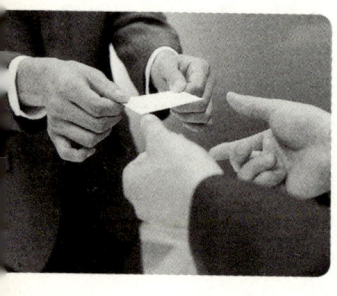

MEETINGS

It is important to be well prepared and to plan business discussions in great detail before meetings. Not only is punctuality[2] vital, but it is a good idea to arrive fifteen minutes before the scheduled time. Members of a team might come from different

ethnic groups, and so, although the Chinese will shake hands upon greeting, Muslims and Malays may prefer salaams, that is, putting their hands together and giving a slight bow saying "*salaam,*" or "peace." Similarly, Hindus might use the same form saying "*namaste.*" Business meetings are usually conducted in English.

Tea is always served at meetings and it is polite to accept it. You will notice that the seating is hierarchical and the visitor will be seated next to the host. Dress is usually more formal than it would be in the office and shorts are most definitely not worn. Expect meetings to be rather slow. Although the Chinese issue agendas and stick to them, they tend to have a rather verbose[1] negotiating style; also, in Asia generally it is considered important and polite to pause for about fifteen seconds before answering a question or considering a statement. This is longer than is the norm in the West, but it does not mean that the feeling is negative. Singaporeans look for "how" you say things as well as "what" you say, and decision-making happens slowly. If all this seems

[1] 详细的，冗长的

[1] 畏缩的，气馁的
[2] （此处指）受益
[3] 暗示，提示

a little daunting[1], remember that once made, decisions will hold good for the long term, and Asian businesspeople do not like being rushed into hasty decisions.

Be patient and allow time for reflection. It is also a good idea to restate your position several times if necessary because polite persistence pays off[2]. Never, of course, let frustration make you lose your temper. A warm, friendly attitude emphasizing common aims will be much more constructive. Remember the golden rule that throughout Asia "yes" does not necessarily mean "I agree" — it is more like "I hear you." Chinese speakers tend to use an indirect style, hinting[3] rather than telling, and sometimes smile to avoid embarrassment when giving bad news.

Always end your meetings with a summary of what was discussed, what was agreed upon, and what actions are to be carried out and by whom.

WOMEN IN BUSINESS

Women are well represented in the professions, commerce, and industry, with many holding senior managerial positions. Western business visitors should always observe Singaporean protocols¹ where dress, behavior in the office, and body language are concerned; any sign of flirting could destroy the woman's position and certainly ruin a business deal. Singaporean women tend to dress conservatively and, despite the hot, humid climate, upper arms are always covered and knee-length² skirts are the norm. In more formal offices women often wear pantyhose³, but not in more relaxed establishments⁴.

SAVING FACE

The all-important issue of "saving face" applies to all three ethnic groups. The point to remember here is that saving face — as with everything in Singapore — is not just about individuals but about the group to which they belong. Losing face is not just a matter of personal embarrassment: it undermines an individual's integrity and moral character. More than that, it undermines the whole group. Most importantly, saving face preserves the group's harmony, whether the group at the

1. 礼节，行为准则
2. 齐膝的
3. 连身裤袜
4. （此处指）公司

Chapter 08

1 犯错，做错，办错
2 （此处指）危险地带
3 敏锐地，巧妙地
4 机智，手法
5 用肘轻推，轻推
6 斥责，指责

time is the family, one's work colleagues, or the nation itself. To embarrass somebody totally or make them lose face is one of the worst mistakes a foreign visitor can make. Asians have long memories. The person who has brought about this loss of face will be regarded as shallow and lacking in personal integrity, and therefore not to be trusted.

So it is important not to blunder[1] inadvertently into this potential minefield[2]. Be very careful about criticism and strong disagreement. If it is essential to be critical, then do so subtly[3] and with tact[4]. When disagreeing with someone, try to nudge[5] them gently in the other direction. Never think that you are being too subtle, for a Singaporean will always get the hint and even respect you for being so aware of the cultural differences between Asia and the West.

Never rebuke[6] a senior in front of a junior, or ask a junior's opinion in front of a senior, or openly praise just one member of the group without including the group as a whole. Within the group they will know who deserves the praise.

Losing one's temper is also seen as a "loss of face," as is any other display of strong emotion — a person who is out of control or reveals their emotions too easily cannot be trusted.

NEGOTIATING STYLES

In Singapore successful outcomes with a partner, customer, or supplier are more likely and certainly easier if you can appreciate how the person across the table or at the other end of the telephone or e-mail is thinking about the business opportunity or the problem to be solved. Asians do not think just in terms of cause and effect, one thing leading to another, but rather in terms of their network of intuitive[1] and intricate[2] relationships and the thought patterns that go with them. The Westerner often enjoys talking about the problem and then the solutions. The Asian wants to know the benefits, certainly the financial benefits but also the impact on relationships within his or her organization and the wider world.

A focus on the benefits of any deal or arrangement and on the common ground

[1] 直觉的
[2] 复杂的，错综的

1 不顾的，无关的
2 合约条款
3 缓解，减轻
4 承担风险，后果自负
5 认可，让步

cannot be stressed too highly. Where there are problems the Asian mind will be prepared to share the burden and will expect this to cut both ways, irreplaceable[1] of any contractual terms[2]. If there are other existing relationships that will be disadvantaged by the deal, it is well to look for ways of mitigation[3] to ease the mind of the person you are negotiating with. This might mean the arrangements are not as clean-cut as you would like, but it is more likely that the deal will fly, especially if the damage is done to someone who has many dealings with the person you are negotiating with.

Any weaknesses you have will be exploited in attempts to reach a decision — disclose them at your peril[4], even if it means that you have to catch the nine o'clock plane home. Know your walking away point, hold to this, and do not make early concessions[5]. Stress the package nature of any concession you offer — there must be something in return. Refer to the pressure you are having from the head office or senior management if you are close to a deal and are having difficulty in closing.

The benefits of having a Singaporean as part of your team are enormous. Not only will they pick up shades of meaning that have passed you by, but they will also discover in the meeting, or more likely outside, the crucial issues to be resolved to reach a settlement.

DECISION MAKING

It is important to know who the decision maker is and what his needs are if it is not the person sitting opposite you. Because the Asian commitment is not just to a contract that has been pored over[1] by the lawyers, but to a relationship, reaching decisions can be slow. However, implementation[2] in Singapore is fast once everything is agreed to.

If a decision seems difficult to achieve, be prepared to table and discuss the benefits and disadvantages to your side as well as the other person, and show how the deal is fair if not ideal.

The one comfort in doing business in Singapore is that it is easier than most Asian countries to negotiate and reach a decision, and that there are no "commissions" or any other side

[1] 审视，熟读
[2] 履行，完成

[1] 逐步上升的
[2] 曲解
[3] 长辈，老资格

payments to be made once a deal is reached.

CONTRACTS AND FULFILLMENT

Both sides expect contracts to be honored and fulfilled. However, the nature of business in Asia is that, in the event of trouble, whether it be escalating[1] raw material costs or a decline in demand, the problem is expected to be shared. Cooperation and flexibility mean that one does not follow the small print of the contract to the letter.

E-mail Contact

Even when you know someone very well it is best to avoid using e-mail except for the exchange of factual data. Once into the area of ideas or concepts or proposals all sorts of misinterpretations[2] are possible in the shorthand style that is so convenient for other purposes.

TEAM BUILDING

Finally we turn to teams and teamwork. As in other areas of life and work in Singapore, seniority[3] as well as professionalism is very important. The team leader makes the decisions after lengthy consultation with the group, so that every member is on board with the decision. Thereafter[1] the team leader demands implicit obedience and it would be unthinkable for a member of the team to complain about the decision. Harmony, again, is all important, and because of this working practice tends to be slow and methodical. The length of the process can sometimes frustrate foreign managers who are used to more rapid decision making, but even so they appreciate the wisdom of taking the time to reach a decision that is fully supported.

The team leader is responsible not only for selecting its members, but for giving clear, concise instructions, emphasizing the collective nature of the enterprise, making certain that everyone is occupied, and regularly monitoring the team's progress. An effective team leader will be aware that a smile does not equal satisfaction, and perhaps more importantly that a statement of agreement does not necessarily mean that a person understands. It is essential to give face to everyone and certainly never criticize a senior in

[1] 其后, 从那时以后

1 挑选

front of the whole team. Only ever comment on poor performance in private. A diligent manager will give encouragement and praise where it is due, but remember to praise the whole team and not single out[1] a particular member, thereby causing embarrassment and loss of face.

Chapter 09

COMMUNICATING

TELECOMMUNICATIONS

There are two telecom companies in Singapore offering the full data and voice, broadband[1]/ multimedia, and e-service range. They are SingTel[2], with hubs in Singapore and Australia, and StarHub[3], owned by Singapore Technologies (ST) and the global players BT[4] and NTT[5].

The international dialing code for Singapore is 0065, but once inside Singapore you will not need any special area dialing codes. However, Singapore has recently added the prefix 6 to all landlines[6] so, if you were given a number some time ago and are having trouble getting through, this could well be the reason.

[1] 宽带
[2] 新加坡电信有限公司，是新加坡最大的电信公司
[3] 新加坡全集成信息通信公司
[4] 英国电信供应商，为全球170多个国家提供电信服务
[5] 日本电报电话公司，成立于1976年，是日本最大的电信服务提供商—日本电信电话株式会社的全资子公司
[6] 固定电话

[1] 货币兑换处
[2] 太平洋商业网络有限公司

Local calls in Singapore cost very little: they are practically free from private phones and cost 10 cents from public phones for three minutes. Many people now use card phones instead of pay phones as well as credit-card phones. Phone cards are widely available from post offices, *bureaux de change*[1], pharmacies, bookstores, and shops such as 7 Eleven. International phone cards are also widely available.

If you want to use your cell phone while in Singapore it is a good idea to check with your provider as to how to do this and how much it will cost.

THE INTERNET

Apart from the telecom companies, the other Internet providers are Pacific Internet[2], the Asia-wide provider, and Reddweb. The easiest and cheapest way to contact friends and family while in Singapore is to use the Internet, and it is practical to sign up for a free Internet e-mail address that you can use anywhere. There are many Internet cafés where you can easily get a line and, as this is

Singapore, most hotels offer in-room modems[1] to their guests. In fact, with over 150 hotspots[2] in the city, getting online at broadband speeds could not be easier.

For those who are going to spend more than a few days in the country, the most useful Web site for information is *www.expatsingapore.com*.

THE MEDIA

The two media groups are SPH[3] (Singapore Press Holdings) and MediaCorp[4] (Media Corporation of Singapore), which publish newspapers and magazines, broadcast on TV, and have comprehensive websites and online editions. MediaCorp also has radio stations. SPH only recently became a broadcaster and MediaCorp similarly only recently entered the newspaper business.

Newspapers and Magazines

Daily newspapers are available in all four official languages, and in English there are the *Straits Times*, the *Business Times*, and the afternoon tabloid[5]

[1] 调制解调器
[2] 热点
[3] 新加坡报业控股有限公司，几乎垄断新加坡国内报章的出版发行业务
[4] 新传媒私人有限公司，新加坡唯一免费电视经营商
[5] 小报

[1] 可提供的内容
[2] 时尚的
[3] 高档的，豪华的
[4] 报摊，杂志摊

the *New Paper*, all owned by SPH, and *Today* owned by MediaCorp.

The *Straits Times* has a broad coverage of local, regional, and international news and its excellent website (*www.straitstimes.asia1.com.sg*) gives the visitor an opportunity to get up to date with the latest news and events. The *Business Times* (*www.businesstimes.asia1.com.sg*) covers the commercial and financial issues in much the same way, while the tabloid *New Paper* is purely for local consumption, as a visit to its website (*www.newpaper.asia1.com.sg*) will demonstrate. *Today* (*www.todayonline.com*) is positioned as a mid-market alternative to the SPH offerings[1].

All papers are sensitive to the government line on major issues and are not controversial.

Of the local magazines, the glossy[2] *Vogue Singapore* will give you an insight and perhaps a taste for the more exclusive[3] side of the island's life.

The international press and magazines are well represented on the newsstands[4] but will disappear if something offends the country's sensitivities[1] or its government.

TV and Radio

All four languages are catered to by MediaCorp and the channels to watch in English are Channel 5 and NewsAsia, while SPH broadcasts TV in Chinese and with the English-language Channel i.

Turning the FM dial will bring you the MediaCorp stations with Gold at 90.5 with news and music, classical music on Symphony at 92.4, NewsRadio at 93.8, old to new hits[2] at Class 95.0, and the latest on Perfect at 98.7.

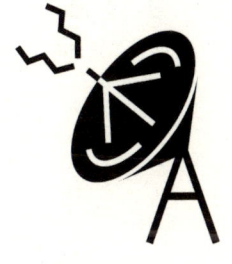

POSTAL SERVICES

Mail is usually delivered by the next working day at some time in early to late afternoon through a network of more than 1,300 postal outlets around the island. Singapore addresses use a six-digit postal code and the basic mail service is run by Singapore Post (SP), a subsidiary[3] of SingTel. SP has the exclusive right to provide basic mail service (letters and postcards) until 2007. Express services (small packets, printed papers, and parcels)

[1] 敏感
[2] 点击量
[3] 子公司

[1] 快递公司
[2] 敦豪国际货运公司，德国邮政下属的国际快递物流公司，与 FedEx, UPS, TNT 为全球四大快递公司
[3] 联邦国际快递，国际性速递集团，总部位于美国田纳西洲
[4] 联合包裹，总部设于美国的国际快递公司
[5] 天地国际速递公司，总部位于荷兰
[6] 散布，分布
[7] 公共设施账单
[8] 通晓、使用多种语言的

have been opened up to competition, and many courier companies[1] offer such services to local and international destinations. The international courier companies such as DHL[2], Fedex[3], UPS[4], and TNT[5] are all found in the city.

In addition Singapore has some distinctive services and these include:

Express LUM, to send urgent local mail anywhere on the island on a same-day basis.

SAMs (self-service automated machines) dotted around[6] the island. Here you can weigh postal items, pay fines and telephone/utility bills[7], and buy stamps at any time, day or night.

Speedpost, an SP international courier service up to 21 kg.

Fastfreight, an SP door-to-door delivery service that sends urgent heavy shipments (over 21 kg) to more than 125 countries worldwide.

LANGUAGES

In 1965 great consideration was given to the question of which language should be the official one in the new polyglot[8] nation. With three distinctive ethnic groups, it was a highly sensitive issue, especially as racial tensions often threatened to explode over minor issues, and, in some cases, actually did so.

In 1959, when Singapore attained self-government, it was all very straightforward: Malay was declared the official language in order to prepare the way for entry into the Federation of Malaysia. All that changed after August 9, 1965, because the Singaporean government realized that if it continued with Malay as the official language the country would not be able to make a living as an international trading community, which was imperative[1] if the new nation were to survive. The Singaporean Chinese now actively promoted Chinese as the new official language, their cultural, business, and civic leaders pointing out to Lee Kuan Yew's government that it was the language spoken by more than 80 percent of the population. The Chinese, understandably, felt proud of their language and culture, and indeed in the 1950s all classes of Chinese in Singapore — from businessmen to rickshaw drivers — gave

[1] 势在必行的，急需的

1. 新加坡南洋大学(1955年–1980年),新加坡华人出资建立的第一所海外华人大学。1980年,南洋大学与新加坡大学合并成立"新加坡国立大学",而留在南洋大学校园内的理工学院时称"南洋理工学院",后来成为"南洋理工大学"的核心部分
2. 分裂的
3. 背叛的行为

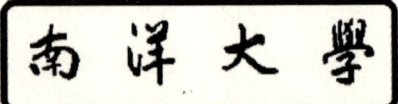

money toward the founding of a Chinese-language university in Singapore that was named "Nantah[1]," which soon became the symbol of Chinese culture and values, language and education.

It seemed to follow that Chinese would become the official language. However, Lee Kuan Yew had other ideas and he concluded that the least divisive[2] solution to this problem would be to have four official languages: Malay, Mandarin Chinese, Tamil, and English. In this way, no one ethnic group would have a linguistic advantage.

Malay was to be the language of administration. But it was not the use of Tamil or Malay as official languages that angered the Chinese community: it was the introduction of English as an official language, especially as it was to be taught in all schools in addition to a child's ethnic language, that was considered a betrayal[3]. Indeed, Lee Kuan Yew and his government were portrayed as "pseudo[1] foreigners who forget their ancestors" in one of the leading Chinese newspapers.

Singapore, however, had a history of excellence in the teaching of subjects in the English language — it had been the regional center for education in English. It had good schools, arts and science colleges, and teacher-training and medical colleges. The brightest English-educated students from Malaya and Borneo[2], as well as the former Dutch East Indies[3] (which later became Indonesia), attended these colleges and trained as doctors, teachers, and other professionals as well as administrators. The opposition to English as one of the common languages was unremitting, especially at Nantah. Eventually, in 1978, Lee Kuan Yew persuaded this institution to make English the language of instruction. The majority of the Chinese-speaking parents accepted this change as inevitable, as did the students — especially because graduates were having great difficulty in finding employment compared to their fellow students who had been educated in English at the University of Singapore. Although

[1] 假的
[2] 婆罗洲岛，位于马来半岛东南部，世界第三大岛，世界上唯一的分属于三个国家（印度尼西亚、马来西亚和文莱）的岛屿
[3] 荷属东印度，指 1800 至 1949 年为荷兰人所统治的印度尼西亚，1949 年作为印度尼西亚独立

[1] 福建人
[2] 客家人,就是外来人的意思
[3] 河洛人,中国南方操闽南方言的群体,主要分布在福建、粤东和台湾等地,另外在新加坡、泰国和马来西亚等地华侨也是河洛人的后代
[4] 福州人

it was a painful adjustment for Nantah to make, by the early 1990s Nantah and the University of Singapore felt confident enough to merge and become the National University of Singapore, or NUS as it is now known.

However, the language debate was still not over — although this time it was the status of the Chinese language or, more precisely, the different Chinese dialects that are still spoken in Singapore reflecting the many regions where the immigrants originated. The predominant ones are Hokkien[1], Hakka[2], Hainanese, Hoklo[3], Hokchiu[4], and, to a lesser extent, Cantonese (the latter being the dialect spoken in Hong Kong). From the 1980s onward, Prime Minister Lee Kuan Yew encouraged the speaking of Mandarin in the home because he realized it would be easier for children to master it at school if they were not burdened by dialects. He therefore stopped making speeches in his native Hokkien, and TV and radio program makers were no longer permitted to broadcast in Chinese dialects, only in Mandarin. To encourage the speaking of the language the Prime Minister instituted a "speak Mandarin" day once a month.

At first, the insistence on the use of Mandarin was seen by many Singaporean Chinese as something of an academic exercise: all very well in theory, but making no difference to the practical issues of the day, such as making money. However, the opening up of China, whose official language has always been Mandarin, brought about a swift change of attitude. It soon became clear that those in the workforce, whether professional or technical, could command a premium if they spoke Mandarin as well as English. The handing back of Hong Kong to China in 1997 further underlined the importance of Mandarin because the Singaporean Chinese could see their fellow overseas Chinese having to embrace it. Mandarin has always been the language of government and administration, and, indeed, for centuries the sign of an educated person was that he spoke Mandarin.

Chapter 09

[1] 新加坡式英语，通用于新加坡，指英国英语在当地受到美国英语、福建话、普通话、马来语等影响呈现出混合语的特征
[2] 荒废
[3] 唆使，煽动

Singlish[1]

The Singaporeans have developed their own way of speaking English, known as "Singlish." This is a usage that has its roots in Chinese grammatical structure. Thus the Singlish "You follow me" means "We go together." "Can or not?" means "Will you or won't you?" Moreover, Singaporeans often mix ethnic terms with English words to create more colorful expressions when they feel that the Chinese or Malay word better describes what they want to say.

The government, on the other hand, wants English to be the common bond between all Singaporeans and opposes anything that it sees as the "dumbing down[2]" of the English language, and so, from time to time, it instigates[3] a "speak proper English" campaign.

To the untrained ear, listening to a conversation in rapid "Singaporean" is highly confusing and totally illogical. Overleaf are some examples.

SOME SINGAPOREAN PHRASES

Boh-chup from the Hokkien meaning "could not be bothered/could not care less" e.g., "Ah, boh-chup — I didn't win the lottery."

Havoc from the English "disorder," or "confusion," but used here as an adjective: "My son is so havoc he doesn't do his homework and wants to go to clubs!"

Kayu from the Malay meaning "stupid": "My son is so kayu, he always gets poor grades at school."

Lah a Malay prefix used to emphasize something, as in: "He can do it lah, no problem," or "No lah," meaning "no way."

Maama from the Tamil word for uncle, so a "Maama shop" is an Indian/English word meaning a shop run by an Indian merchant.

Obiang from the Hokkien word meaning ugly: "That dress is so obiang."

Uwee this is derived from Australian slang meaning a "U-turn": "I'll have to do a uwee."

Waah! has no precise meaning, but is an exclamation of excitement and amazement. This word is frequently heard at banquets as each new dish appears.

Even when using the English language, which we know has been taught in Singapore schools for over thirty years, mistakes and confusion can arise. If you find the way in which something is said upsetting, remember that for none of the ethnic groups is English their first language, and even

[1] 模糊

when speaking it they will often still use their own grammatical structure. Something that would be perfectly polite in Chinese can sound abrupt and offensive when translated literally into English. For example, in the West we say to a guest "Would you like a cup of tea?" In Singapore this becomes "You want to drink tea or not?"!

Similarly, in Chinese and Malay there are no tense changes, they simply use a time phrase to indicate past or future. Again, to a foreigner this can sound very uneducated when it is directly translated into English. For example, "I see that movie already with my friend."

The tip here is to be culturally sensitive and not immediately to jump to the conclusion that somebody is being deliberately rude. Learn to tolerate ambiguity[1], and accept a degree of frustration in order to deal with the different circumstances you will encounter.

BODY LANGUAGE

Westerners often find it difficult to read a Singaporean's body language, although they have no problem in understanding their Western counterparts[1], who are used to being more direct. Westerners may find it difficult to conceal anger, frustration, boredom, or tiredness, and recognize these signs in others. However, in a culture where harmony is promoted and people do not want to give bad news, body language can be much more difficult to interpret. We have seen in the chapter on business that in all three ethnic groups "Yes" does not necessarily mean "I agree." If there is a slight pause, an embarrassed smile, or a sucking[2] through the teeth, this probably means that "Yes" is "No." The Indian community adds another dimension to body language in the matter of "Yes" and "No." An Indian will wag[3] his head, which to the Westerner can look like a "No," when he is actually replying in the affirmative[4].

In some other countries, you might encounter loud belching after a meal, or spitting in the street, but not nose-blowing. You should be aware that all these actions are considered equally disgusting in Singapore, by all groups. If you have a cold

1 与对方地位相当的人，同仁
2 吮吸
3 摇摆
4 肯定的，同意的

1 （用布）擦去，揩干（汗水）
2 双关
3 自嘲的，自贬的；谦虚的
4 职业道德
5 闹剧

and need to blow your nose, you should excuse yourself from the present company and go to the bathroom to do so. You might notice that there are large handkerchiefs for sale in the shops, but these are intended for mopping[1] your brow in the most humid months.

HUMOR

Humor, especially British humor, does not work well as it relies heavily on puns[2] and is often self-deprecating[3]. So, if a Singaporean asks you "How many people work in your company?" and you reply "About half," your Singaporean colleague will think that the employees are lazy and the company must surely go bankrupt. Even if you smile when saying this, remember that in Singapore this could be a sign that you are embarrassed by the lack of the work ethic[4] in your company — not that you are not to be taken seriously.

The Chinese, Indians, and Malays do have a sense of humor, but it tends to be more of the slapstick[5] variety.

CONCLUSION

E. M. Forster[1] famously said that the first person you meet when you go abroad is yourself. Once outside the familiar boundaries of your own culture, your sense of self is challenged. This is partly what makes foreign travel so exciting. It is a learning experience that can be both interesting and demanding[2], and it can be a revelation[3] to discover how you act and think in unfamiliar situations. If some of the many dos and don'ts listed here seem a little daunting[4] — relax. The Singaporeans understand that you are a stranger in their land and will not expect you to be familiar with their customs, but they will be delighted if you attempt to learn something about their culture. This guide will set you on the road toward a fuller appreciation of this uniquely rich and varied society.

[1] 爱德华·摩根·福斯特(1879-1970)，20世纪英国著名作家
[2] 要求高的
[3] 显示
[4] 令人畏惧的

APPENDICES

PLACES

Arabian Peninsula
阿拉伯半岛,位于亚洲。沙特阿拉伯、卡塔尔、伊拉克等国位于阿拉伯半岛上

Batam
巴丹岛,是印尼距新加坡最近的一个岛屿

Bengal
孟加拉,南亚国家,位于孟加拉湾北部

Bintan
民丹岛,是印尼寥内群岛的最大岛屿,由于位置接近赤道,因此终年阳光普照,是高尔夫球爱好者的好去处

Bornco
婆罗洲岛,位于马来半岛东南部,世界第三大岛,世界上唯一的分属于三个国家(印度尼西亚、马来西亚和文莱)的岛屿

Bugis
武吉士,地铁站名。位于新加坡中心地带,是著名的购物、美食和社交场所

Bukit Timah Hill
武吉知马山,新加坡海拔最高点,热带雨林保护区

Changi airport
新加坡樟宜机场,是新加坡主要的民用机场和亚洲重要的航空枢纽

Appendices

Changi jail
樟宜监狱，位于新加坡东部樟宜地区，1942 年新加坡被日本占领后曾被日军用来关押俘虏

Dutch East Indies
荷属东印度，指 1800 至 1949 年为荷兰人所统治的印度尼西亚，1949 年作为印度尼西亚独立

Eastern Siberia
东西伯利亚

Fort Siloso
西乐索炮台，位于圣淘沙西乐索海滩近山处

four river deltas
四个三角洲，分别指流入福州的闽江，厦门的九龙江，汕头附近的韩江以及位于广州南部的珠江

Indonesian archipelago
印度尼西亚群岛，世界上最大的群岛，包含 17,000 多个岛屿，从印度洋的苏门答腊岛直至太平洋的哈马黑拉岛

Java
爪哇岛，印度尼西亚首都雅加达，位于爪哇岛西北部

Kerala
喀拉拉，位于印度的西南端，渔业极为发达

Kuala Lumpur
吉隆坡，马来西亚首都

Malaya
马来亚，是马来西亚西部的旧称，又名西马来

Manchuria
满洲，我国东北旧称

Mandai Orchid Gardens
万里胡姬花公园，是新加坡最著名的园艺旅游圣地之一，展示了包括新加坡国花在内的多种胡姬花，包括古香花园、水上花园和热带水果园

Marina Bay
位于新加坡南部的滨海湾

Mecca
麦加，座落在沙特阿拉伯西部赛拉特山区，四周群山环抱，层峦起伏，景色壮丽，是伊斯兰教第一圣地

Medina
麦地那，位于沙特阿拉伯国境内，是伊斯兰教的第二圣地，与麦加、耶路撒冷一起被称为伊斯兰教的三大圣地

Mei Lo River
汨罗江，位于湖南省，属洞庭湖水系

Nepal
尼泊尔

Orchard Road
乌节路，新加坡著名的商业旅游街

Penang
（马来西亚）槟城

Pulau Ubin Islands
乌敏岛，位于新加坡东北部，主要由花岗岩组成，因此开采花岗岩是岛内主要的经济活动

Sentosa Island
圣淘沙岛

Serangoon Road
实龙岗路，新加坡最古老的马路之一

Appendices

St. John's Island
圣约翰岛，曾为监狱，现成为著名的旅游景点

Straits of Malacca
马六甲海峡，位于马来西亚和苏门答腊之间，现由新加坡、马来西亚和印度尼西亚三国共同管辖

Suez Canal
苏伊士运河，地理位置极为重要，是亚洲、非洲和欧洲往来的主要通道，连接地中海与红海

Sumatra
苏门答腊，印度尼西亚第二大岛屿，东北隔马六甲海峡与马来半岛相望。自古以来苏门答腊山区出产黄金，因此也被称为金洲

Swatow
汕头

Syonan
新加坡1942年沦陷时被日本称为昭南岛

Tamil Nadu
泰米尔纳德邦，位于印度南部

the Malay Peninsula
马来半岛，又叫克拉半岛或马六甲半岛，位于亚洲东南部。马来半岛包括泰国的西南部、马来西亚的西部和新加坡，自古以来是联系经济和文化的枢纽

the River Kwai
桂河，新加坡著名的旅游景点

the Rochor River
梧槽河，源头在武吉知马，位于新加坡加冷

the Sungei Buloh Wetland Reserve
双溪布洛湿地保护区，位于新加坡西北部，占地87公顷，是重要的自然

保护区，也是唯一受保护的沼泽自然公园，独特的候鸟群是其特色之一

the USSR
是 the Union of Soviet Socialist Republics 的缩写，指前苏联

Tioman
刁曼岛，位于马来西亚东部，由 64 个小岛组成的火山群岛之中最大的一个，是新加坡人喜爱的旅游去处之一

PEOPLE

Ava Gardner (1922–1990)
艾娃·加德纳，美国著名女演员

Confucius (公元前 551 年 – 公元前 478 年)
孔子，中国古代著名思想家、教育家，开创了私人讲学的风气，是儒家学派的创始人

Elizabeth Taylor (1932–2011)
伊丽莎白·泰勒，著名好莱坞女演员

E. M. Forster (1879–1970)
爱德华·摩根·福斯特，20 世纪英国著名作家

George Coleman (1795–1844)
乔治·科尔曼，爱尔兰著名建筑师

Joseph Conrad (1857–1924)
约瑟夫·康拉德，出生在波兰，30 岁时开始学习英语，后成为著名的用非母语写作的小说家

Le Corbusier (1887–1965)
勒·柯布西耶，20 世纪最著名的法国建筑师，城市规划家

Lee Kuan Yew (1923–2015)
李光耀是新加坡首任总理,新加坡人民行动党创始人之一,被誉为"新加坡国父",对新加坡政治影响力巨大。李光耀有着良好的教育背景,1935年考入莱佛士书院初中部,在日军占领新加坡后中断学业,1946年留学英国,在伦敦经济学院学习,后转入剑桥大学学习法律,于1949年考获双重一等荣誉学位,取得律师资格。李光耀在1965年新加坡独立后积极倡导经济改革与发展,支持人才强国,主张高薪养廉和文明的生活习惯,对目前新加坡发展成为一个花园国家有着重要作用

Lim Bo Seng (1909–1944)
林谋盛,新加坡开拓者之一

Lord Hastings (1732–1818)
沃伦·黑斯廷斯,英国殖民地官员,在印度等多地任职

Marco Polo (1254–1324)
马可波罗,13世纪意大利著名的商人和旅行家

prophet Muhammad (约 570–632)
先知穆罕默德,政治家、宗教领袖,穆斯林认可的伊斯兰先知

Qu Yuan (公元前 340 年 – 公元前 278 年)
屈原,战国时期楚国的辞赋家,后投汨罗江而死

Rudyard Kipling (1865–1936)
拉迪亚德·吉卜林,英国著名小说家、诗人,出生于印度,代表作有《丛林故事》等

Siddhartha Gautama (公元前 563 年 – 公元前 483 年)
悉达多·乔达摩,佛教创始者,被后世尊称为释迦牟尼佛

Somerset Maugham (1874–1965)
萨默塞特·毛姆,英国著名小说家、戏剧家,其代表作《月亮和六便士》描写的是一个英国画家来到南太平洋后与土著人共同生活的故事

Sultan Hussein of Johore (1776–1835)
新加坡的马来国王

Sun Yat Sen (1866–1925)
孙中山,中国近代伟大的资产阶级革命先行者

Teo Eng Hock (1872–1957)
张永福,生于新加坡,孙中山辛亥革命时在海外的主要助手

Thomas Stamford Raffles (1781–1826)
托马斯·斯坦福·莱佛士,为英国殖民时期东印度群岛的行政官员,新加坡海港城市的创建人,主要贡献在于将新加坡建立为欧洲和亚洲间的重要国际港口

William Wilberforce (1759–1833)
威廉·威尔伯福斯,英国政治家,英国反对奴隶贸易的领导人

EXERCISES

Chapter 01 Land & People

❶ Choose the most appropriate answer from the four choices according to the information in the passage.

1) Singapore is hot and _____ all year round as it has a typical tropical climate.
   A. sticky   B. chilly
   C. scalding   D. foggy

2) _____ refers to the act of deliberately damaging public property.
   A. Conviction   B. Burglary
   C. Vandalism   D. Pickpocket

3) Most large corporations have cash reserves as a _____ for bad times.
   A. strategy   B. contingency
   C. measure   D. mishap

4) As the _____ deepened, more people become jobless.
   A. recession   B. reform
   C. prosperity   D. corruption

5) A well-organized group is bound to be a _____ one and all people are dedicated to one goal.
   A. concentrated   B. coherent
   C. conclusive   D. cohesive

★ 答案请到中国外语网（www.cflo.com.cn）"教师资源"板块查询下载。

❷ Answer the following questions according to the passage in the fewest possible words.
1) What kinds of action would incur heavy fines?
2) What kind of campaign did the Singapore government take against low population growth?
3) Who has the most influence on Singapore in making Singapore into the Asian powerhouse?

❸ Think critically and answer the following questions.
1) Why is Singapore a land of immigrants?
2) What have you learned from Singapore's history?

Chpater 02 Values & Attitudes

❶ Choose the most appropriate answer from the four choices according to the information in the passage.
1) Singapore prides itself on being a meritocracy and in the last thirty years this merit has come very much to the _____.
   A. stage   B. fore
   C. prominence   D. point
2) Hinduism embraces lots of apparent _____, differing forms of worship, and a profusion of divinities superficially.
   A. contradictions   B. resemblances
   C. similarities   D. reverences
3) If people feel like a fish out of water, we consider him as a social _____.

A. displacement B. mishap
   C. detachment D. misfit
4) Singaporeans give _____ to age and learning as they believe age and learning can bring wisdom.
   A. deference B. obedience
   C. adherence D. preference
5) Children are taught never to _____ the group or bring shame upon their family.
   A. defer B. twist
   C. dishonor D. venerate

❷ Think critically and answer the following questions.
1) The Chinese, Malays and Inidans in Singapore believe in different religions. Try to state the core of one of the religions you are familiar with.
2) Give some examples to illustrate that Singapore is a goal-driven society.

Chapter 03 Customs & Traditions

❶ Read the following statements and decide whether they are true or false. Write T if the statement is true and F if it is false.
1) Unlike Chinese and Malays, the Indians open presents in front of the giver. (   )
2) There are different kinds of traditions due to the fact that Singapore mainly consists of Chinese, Malays and Indians. (   )

3) New Chinese mothers are often forbidden to go outdoors for the first month after giving birth to a baby. ( )
4) Singaporeans are very westernized, so they don't observe lots of traditional beliefs including ancient Chinese astrology. ( )
5) The Festival of Lights, or Deepavali, is celebrated at the darkest time of the year by means of lighting oil lamps and dragon dance. ( )

❷ Complete the sentences with the information given in the passage.
1) The third day of Chinese New Year in Singapore is _____ remembering and venerating the ancestors, so friends don't visit each other.
2) The _____ of the Mongol Yuan Dynasty by Chinese rebels became the legend associated with mooncakes.
3) Most Malay children's name are formally _____ on him or her forty-four days after birth.
4) The ringing of bells and shouts and chants of Hindu wedding ceremony are intended to keep evil spirits at _____.

❸ Think critically and answer the following questions.
1) What are the differences among Chinese weddings, Malay weddings and Hindu ones?
2) Give an account of superstitions you have learned about Chinese living in Singapore when they give gifts and tell whether Chinese around you have such superstitions.

Chapter 04 The Singaporeans at home

❶ Choose the most appropriate answer from the four choices according to the information in the passage.

1) Foreigners in Singapore are _____ to hear "Auntie" or "Uncle" used by children in unlikey circumstances.
   A. terrified   B. bemused
   C. adoring   D. worried

2) As Chinese attach great importance to family, it comes as no surprise that the family name is given _____ in the order of an individual's name.
   A. preference   B. importance
   C. consideration   D. precedence

3) _____ people live in large, luxurious private apartments complete with swimming pools.
   A. Affluent   B. Deprived
   C. Ordinary   D. Impoverished

4) English is not only a _____ to economic success, but also it serves as a common language.
   A. trigger   B. clue
   C. conduit   D. cue

5) The left hand is not used when people eat, shake hands or give gifts in Malay or Indian households, as it is reserved for personal _____.
   A. hygiene   B. health
   C. symbol   D. indication

❷ Think critically and answer the following questions.
1) Is there any difference between Singapore and Chinese in the ways of marriage? Try to give some examples.
2) What do you know about names of Indians?

Chapter 05 Food & Drink

❶ Choose the most appropriate answer from the four choices according to the information in the passage.

1) The _____ of culinary traditions began in Singapore's earliest days which blended Chinese, Malay and Indian cuisines.
   A. mixture   B. fusion
   C. influx   D. variations

2) Chinese tea is the normal _____ to a meal as tea is believed to prevent obesity and help digestion.
   A. accompaniment   B. accompany
   C. accomplice   D. accomplishment

3) Barbecuing and grilling soon joined Chinese stir-frying, braising, and steaming _____.
   A. technologies   B. techniques
   C. culinary traditions   D. culinary styles

4) _____ skin must be protected from the sun especially in summer.
   A. Succulent   B. Leafy
   C. Fragile   D. Delicate

5) A majority of northern Chinese prefer noodles because the climate is too _____ to grow rice.
   A. enlivened   B. hearty
   C. severe   D. favorable

❷ Think critically and answer the following questions.
   1) List some of the cooking styles in Singapore and try to give some examples.
   2) What are the differences between Chinese and Singaporeans when it comes to drinks?

Chapter 06 Time Out

❶ Answer the following questions according to the passage in the fewest possible words.
   1) What are the most famous tourist attractions in Singapore?
   2) Is tourism a prosperous industry in Singapore?
   3) What are the advantages of MRT?

❷ Think critically and answer the following questions.
   1) Can you describe the means of transportation for visitors in Singapore?
   2) What tips will you offer to visitors who first come to Singapore?

Chapter 07 Banquets & Entertaining

❶ Read the following statements and decide whether they are true or false. Write T if the statement is true and F if it is false.

1) It is permissible to put your chopsticks upright in a bowl of rice or rest your chopsticks on the rest stand. ( )
2) It is customary for the host to take his seat before everyone else takes theirs. ( )
3) Singaporeans will feel comfortable if entertained "Singapore style". ( )
4) Generally speaking, Muslims do not eat pork or drink alcohol and Indians are often vegetarian. ( )
5) Forks, knives and spoons are usually provided for a meal as meat has to be cut into bite-sized portions. ( )
6) Among traditional Hindus and Muslims, the left hand is not used to touch food. ( )

❷ Think critically and answer the following questions.

1) What are the differences between Chinese and Malays in terms of eating etiquette?
2) Suppose you are a secretary of a company, please share the tips with your colleagues on how to entertain guests after your guests come to a restaurant.

Chapter 08 Business Briefing

❶ Choose the most appropriate answer from the four choices according to the information in the passage.

1) The _____ of immigrants contributed to economic growth in the past decade.
   A. inflection   B. infliction
   C. inflation   D. influx

2) The nations managed to ride _____ the financial crisis with the help of neighboring countries.
   A. on   B. out
   C. around   D. up

3) Singaporeans prefer to get to know business counterparts, so do not _____ into business when first beginning a meeting.
   A. plunge   B. involve
   C. squeeze   D. force

4) Business confidence was _____ by a series of failures.
   A. built   B. established
   C. undermined   D. disclosed

5) Sometimes in order to conclude a contract, both parties have to make some _____.
   A. concessions   B. obligations
   C. offers   D. Benefits

6) After being _____ over by lawyers, the contract can be implemented fast in Singapore.

A. thought B. examined
C. polished D. Pored

7) _____ easily occur in the shorthand style when we write an E-mail, so it is _____ to avoid using E-mail except for the exchange of factual data.

A. Misrepresentation, advisable

B. Misinterpretations, imperative

C. Misinterpretations, advisable

D. Misrepresentations, imperative

❷ Think critically and answer the following questions.

1) How does Asian negotiating style differ from western one in general?
2) What are the tips for doing business with Malays and Indians in terms of hands? Suppose you are a businessman in Singapore, try to offer some tips for your colleagues who are newcomers.

Chapter 09 Communicating

❶ Complete the sentences with the information given in the passage.

1) There are four official languages which are Malay, Mandarin Chinese, _____ and English. This fact shows that Singapore is a _____ nation.
2) The Indian community has a different notion from westerners in terms of body language. If an Indian wags his head, he is actually saying in the _____ while he _____ his head, he is implying he won't agree.

3) In order to be culturally _____, one has to learn to tolerate ambiguity. Something that is very decent in Chinese might be _____ when translated into English.
4) Daily newspapers in Singapore are _____ in all four official languages among which the *Straits Times* has a very broad _____ of both local and international news.

❷ **Think critically and answer the following questions.**
1) How many kinds of communicating ways can you think of in today's world? And try to tell the advantages and disadvantages of the two most frequently used ways when you contact your friends.
2) Have you experienced any culture shock? And try to analyze the reasons.

郑重声明

高等教育出版社依法对本书享有专有出版权。任何未经许可的复制、销售行为均违反《中华人民共和国著作权法》,其行为人将承担相应的民事责任和行政责任;构成犯罪的,将被依法追究刑事责任。为了维护市场秩序,保护读者的合法权益,避免读者误用盗版书造成不良后果,我社将配合行政执法部门和司法机关对违法犯罪的单位和个人进行严厉打击。社会各界人士如发现上述侵权行为,希望及时举报,本社将奖励举报有功人员。

反盗版举报电话　　(010) 58581999　58582371　58582488
反盗版举报传真　　(010) 82086060
反盗版举报邮箱　　dd@hep.com.cn
通信地址　　北京市西城区德外大街4号
　　　　　　高等教育出版社法律事务与版权管理部
邮政编码　　100120